Don't Write Your

MEmoir

Without

ME!

Viga Boland, B.A

My sincerest thanks to the writers, editors and teachers whose words and works have been quoted, with permission, in this book.

SPECIAL THANKS to

BARBARA STUDHAM, HEATHER LAMB and DENIS LEDOUX

For beta reading and encouragement

To HEATHER LAMB for proofreading & feedback

To ANDREW RUDD of http://www.detailfordesign.com

For layout and Book Cover design

ISBN: 978-0-9920497-5-1
ISBN-13: 978-0-9920497-6-8

DEDICATION

This book is dedicated to my family and friends who first encouraged me to write my own memoirs. Without you, and those who subsequently attended my memoir writing workshops at Hamilton Public Library in Ontario and kept asking me to write a "how-to write memoir" book, delivered as closely as possible to the way in which I facilitate memoir writing in those workshops, this book would never have been written. This book is written in honor of you and the loyal members of my MEMOIRABILIA group on Facebook. I hope **"Don't Write Your MEmoir without ME"** will inspire and motivate you to write your memoir at last.

CONTENTS

NOTA BENE

"Your Memoir is a Selfie in Words" (Viga Boland)

If you want to write fiction, read fiction

If you want to write memoir, read memoir

*"Unless you bring a beating heart to your message,
it is dead" (author unknown)*

According to Stephen King:

"If you don't have time to read, you don't have the time (or the tools) to write."

"I'm convinced that fear is at the root of most bad writing."

1 WRITING WITH ABANDONMENT

Don't write your memoir without ME!

Am I being arrogant? Who the heck am I to tell you not to write your memoir without ME?

Wait! Don't toss this book aside just yet. Breathe. I'm not some arrogant know-it-all.

I'm the one who wants to read your memoir because I'm hoping the story you have to share is about me. Well, actually about you. But about me too.

Confused?

Let me explain.

Over the past five years, I've read dozens of memoirs. A handful have been excellent; the majority okay; and the balance? Sigh...

What makes that handful excellent?

They're written by someone who knows MEmoir starts with "ME". If there's no ME in the memoir, no down to earth, regular, ordinary human being who is vulnerable, has weaknesses, thinks things that makes some blush, wants to do things they've been taught not to...in short, doesn't eat, breathe, fart, scream, act out, swear, apologize, trip over themselves, back peddle, say the wrong thing at the wrong time, then there's no "ME" in your memoir. And I'm not interested in reading it!

Now, if you believe your story is one that needs to be told, and that people want to hear, then you need to put yourself 100% into your memoir.

The very word MEmoir starts with "ME"

That is, you! The real you. Warts and all. Not the you who hesitates every time the story becomes too painful, or stops writing when the words reveal something unpleasant about the you behind the mask. Not the you who hits "delete" a second later because you just couldn't let readers know you thought THAT, said THAT, did THAT!

No, no, no! If you're going to write about that masked pretender who needs to be seen in the best light...the sinless, perfect, not fully human person behind the words on the page...DON'T!

Why not?

Because we mere mortals can't relate to that person. We're human and far from perfect. And if you write the masked pretender into your story, your memoir won't resonate with my imperfectly tuned inner self, because I need to know I'm not alone in my imperfection.

It's not that misery loves company. It's that misery loves honesty.

Are you getting where I'm going with this yet?

In short, it's here: if you write your memoir without "me", why would I want to read it?

Oh boy. I can hear you sighing already. I can hear you saying *"What? She wants me to air all the dirty laundry about my life, our family. Exactly the way it happened? Forget it! No way. I don't want to be ostracized..."*

Did I say that? Not at all. Where I'm coming from is more about HOW you write your memoir, and less about WHAT you write.

You see, most folks who decide to write memoir get stuck in the first sentence on the first page. Why? Well, the answer to that is a two-pronged fork. I'll get to the second prong later, but let's look at the first prong for now.

That first prong was jabbed into them by all those well-meaning teachers they had years ago in English composition class. Remember them? They were the ones who knew all the rules of writing (well they did back in the 50's...not so sure about the 70's), who insisted you follow those rules at all times, but had themselves never written anything more creative than an essay for which, by the way, they received an "A".

But, memoir starts with ME. There! I've said it again. And if you have to stop to rewrite that opening line, to replace that word with a better one, to decide if you need a period here, or a semicolon there, or try to remember why you can't start a sentence with "because", "but" or "and" you'll never get that first page written!

Oh, you say. *"She's talking about something else altogether in this book on memoir writing."*

Yes, I am.

I'm talking about writing a book that will earn you an "A", an A for "Abandonment"; a book written by abandoning everything you learned about writing, even everything you've already read in all those other books on memoir writing. I want you to forget all of that.

For now.

I want you to give yourself permission to just write.

Just write because that's the best way, and the only way to put ME into your MEmoir and end up with a memoir the rest of us want to read.

Not sure you can do that? Let me assure you, you can. It just takes a little practice and before long you'll find there's no easier way to get that story out of you and onto the page.

How can I say that with such certainty? Let me fill you in.

2 WHO AM I?

I'm Viga Boland, and I've written four memoirs the way I'm suggesting you should write your memoir.

In fact, I'm writing this book that way too. After all, I believe in practising what I preach.

I'm writing this without thinking how this sounds, or reads to those with a Masters in English Literature. I'm just letting what comes into my head drop right onto the page.

This is what I call writing with Abandonment: not stopping to re-read what I just wrote; not stopping to see if it makes sense; not stopping to even think where should I go next.

Ridiculous?

Not really.

You see, when I write this way, it's easy. EASY!

Stopping, editing, thinking and rethinking is hard. It slows me down. It interrupts my unbridled thoughts. It's as bad as having my husband walk into my room while I'm lost in my writing and ask me a question...which, by the way, he just did now.

Ugh! Talk about killing the flow.

"Well, that's all fine for you," you say, *"but is what you write worth reading when you're done?"*

You tell me: are you still reading?

Okay, I'll stop being cheeky. Let's get serious. The answer is YES. It works.

How do I know that for sure?

Well, when I began writing my first memoir, **"No Tears for my Father"**... on a very difficult subject in which I disclosed an ugly family secret hidden for over 40 years...getting started was the hardest part.

I thought and re-thought how to begin. Days went by as I pondered:

Do I begin at the beginning of my life?

How about at the big moment when walls caved in on my life, right in the middle of things, the way clever novelists hook us? Should I start there?

Maybe I should I open with description: "it was a dark and gloomy night..."

Nah! Perhaps it would be better to start with dialogue e.g. "Come to daddy," my father coaxed. I froze...

I tried all approaches and at the end of three weeks I didn't even have one page written!

"How's your book coming?" my daughter asked. *"How many chapters have you done?"*

How many ways can you tell your daughter to shut up without being offensive?

The truth is, her question gave me just the nudge I needed. I thought back to the days when I used to run motivational workshops for salespeople. I remembered telling them to make a to-do list, and then tackle each job in order of priority.

And then I'd laugh, and tell them to ignore what I had just told them. Why? Because you see, it doesn't really matter where you start.

All that matters is starting!

Anywhere!

Just start!

You figure out the order later on. The only thing that matters is starting.

Now, I'm not the only one who advocates this approach. **Denis Ledoux** of **The Memoir Network**, says:

"Start anywhere in the story you feel like writing about on any given day and keep writing as long as possible."

Remembering what I told those salespeople, I took my own advice. I wrote the first thing that came into my head. I stopped THINKING. I just kept writing. Words expanded into lines. Lines filled pages.

Ten months later, I had a book of 67,000 words and 297 pages.

And I'd written the entire book by abandoning everything I'd ever learned about how to write.

I had stopped THINKING about HOW to write and WHAT to write. I just wrote.

And when my ugly life story had been told, and the world got to read it, the most awesome thing happened: readers wrote to me saying how they cried for me, felt my pain...that as shocking as my story had been, they felt like they had lived it, been right there and had really come to know ME.

Wow!

I couldn't have felt better about my memoir if I'd won a Pulitzer for it. I didn't. But I did get a Gold Medal in the 2014 Readers Favorite Book Awards.

Since that first book, as I said, I have written three more memoirs, taught memoir writing workshops for two years in my local library, and I currently maintain an online blogging website for memoir writers called *Memoirabilia*.

But the best part of all this is now seeing my method works for others who are willing to give writing with abandonment a try. It's seeing them write and publish their own books using what I'm now sharing with you.

According to James Scott Bell, author of many books on writing,

"The best writing comes when you put down words with a certain abandon."

In fact, Scott takes this concept even further. He says:

"Go on writing sprints. That's where you write so fast you don't let your brain assess what you put on the page. At all. Your goal is to over-write, just pour yourself out on the page...let your wild writer's mind run free, and you'll see nuggets coming up to the surface . Edit later and use what you will."

(©James Scott Bell: Voice: The Secret Power of Great Writing)

Are you willing to give "writing with abandonment" to help you put ME into your MEmoir a shot?

Then read on.

3 WHY THIS BOOK?

Good question.

So is this one: *"What about all the other books out there? Surely they offer tons of great advice too?"*

You bet they do. And I'm including a list of those I consulted at the end of this book.

In fact, when I first began running workshops, I purchased at least half a dozen of those other books. I scoured them for info on how to get started writing a memoir. After all, my approach had worked for me, but now I'd committed to helping others write memoir.

All these books contained important information on how to organize your memories, by using "decade timelines". They all suggested remembering the first time you did something, the last time you did something, or saw someone you loved, or tried something you'd never done before.

All great memory prompts, all designed to get you remembering and thinking.

I bought more books; wonderful books by highly qualified authors. They reminded me of everything I'd been taught at school: use description, appeal to the senses, incorporate dialogue. They warned to avoid cliches and not overuse adverbs; to keep a dictionary and Thesaurus handy; and to be prepared to edit, edit, edit.

I went into that first workshop armed with info I didn't have or use while I was writing my first memoir! Heck, I hadn't even read a book about how to write memoir before I wrote mine. The only preparation I'd done before writing mine was to read a couple of others on the same subject, just to see how they dealt with the nitty-gritty and how much they revealed.

But now I knew so much more about writing memoir than I did

before, thanks to those books. I drew up my lesson plans. The English teacher I'd once been was at home with this stuff. All I had to do now was show, teach or remind others how to do it.

Right?

Wrong!

When I first began telling participants about how to organize their memories using "decade timelines", as recommended in those books, I saw their faces light up. They were having those wonderful "AHA" moments. I felt great.

When I pointed out the difference between memoir, autobiography and biography...yes, there is a difference...they realized which of those they really had in mind to write. Knowing that difference is important. Good. We were getting somewhere. This was all working.

And just as the books had prompted, I too suggested they write about a first date; that first day in high school; getting that first job; leaving home; their first marriage (many have more than one); their divorce (first and last); the birth of their first child etc etc., I could almost see the memory wheels spinning in their heads and their eyes lighting up in surprise. Their smiles told me they were thinking, *"If that's all there is to it, maybe I can do this!"*

I didn't dare ask them to consider who would be interested in their stories. At this point, that didn't matter. All that mattered to me was getting them to believe they could do it, and getting them writing. And as they bravely shared what they'd written with other members in the group, they relaxed and smiled, buoyed by the encouragement of their peers.

But then came the other stuff all those informative books harped on: set the moods through description; appeal to the senses; reveal characters through action and dialogue. Don't just narrate, narrate, narrate. Show, don't tell.

Suddenly, I noticed their eyes clouding over. They were back in a classroom, feeling uneasy. Was this all over their heads? A bit too much? Too hard? Now I was becoming uncomfortable. This wasn't going as well as I hoped. I knew what they were thinking:

What? This is only memoir. Why can't I just narrate?

What? You want me to include dialogue in the story? That means correct punctuation. I don't know how or what to use where and when!

What? You want me to show, don't tell? What on earth do you mean?

Why are you making this so hard? We just want to write our memoirs. We're not novelists! Why does all that other stuff matter?

As I saw fear and confusion creep into their eyes, and noticed the "homework" assignments weren't being done, I knew that horrid creature called the "the inner critic" (the other prong in that two-pronged fork I mentioned earlier) was ripping the pen from their fingers and replacing confidence with self-doubt.

Except for one or two people, everything I was now sharing from all those expert-written books was eroding any belief they had started to have that they could do this.

They were becoming discouraged.

All the fabulous information in the books...the prompts, the organizational suggestions...had invoked memories, but not a way to start and continue writing a full memoir. I knew once the stimulation, motivation and confidence they'd felt in the workshops was removed, few, if any of them would finish what they hadn't really even started.

One lady came back for the next session and the next. But she'd written nothing in the interim. Others bought some or all the books I'd recommended, studied them and then decided they were too busy with other things to write now anyway. Others said their husbands just yawned away the whole silly idea of their wives writing a memoir.

I got all that. I felt badly for them but at the same time, I felt I'd somehow let them down. I'd shared what others said they should do, but hadn't shown them what had worked for me: **writing with abandonment**.

There had to be a better way to get those who want to write memoir writing memoir. The solution, as I saw it, was to stop studying and stop thinking about **how** to do it. **Just do it: start writing!**

Okay then. So now dear reader, you may well ask *"just who will benefit from, or support this approach to writing?"*

Well obviously, not those who insist upon traditional approaches.

Why do I say that?

Because traditional approaches require thinking, studying, planning, knowing how to use literary devices and making sure you use them before you even begin writing, or at least being aware of them while you are writing. And don't forget that insistence on grammatical correctness.

In fact, I'm sure any traditionalists reading this now are already frowning as they spot my one-word comments (that aren't sentences of course) or the occasional sentence fragment. Tsk, Tsk! I know all the grammar rules too, but I'm not writing an historical epic here. I'm just trying to speak to you on paper as I would in a workshop. So, for what it's worth, let me ask you this: when you're chatting with a friend or to a group, do you always speak in complete sentences? Case closed.

Sorry, but I'm not going to do that because I don't want this book to be another textbook. I don't want you feeling like you're back in school again.

Remember how hard it was trying to keep in mind everything the teacher had told you while you were writing that essay? Remember going back over the sentence you just wrote, wondering if it was a sentence, or if you should replace a word? Remember the panic and increasing heart rate as you worried if what you were writing even made sense and where to go next?

Excruciating, wasn't it!

My problem with that, and I suspect the problem for a lot of those who want to write memoir, is that approach stops us from writing.

It's like being completely caught up in the best part of a movie, (a movie you happen to be writing!) and the power goes off!

Poof! Creative flow stopped midstream.

Yep! After all those years of learning how to do things, and then teaching others what I learned at school, I've come to one conclusion:

Real learning starts with doing.

Yeah, yeah I know you need to know the rules before you can break them.

But consider this: when you studied the handbook on how to drive a car, could you drive the car the minute you got behind the wheel?

No!

You learned to drive by driving.

In fact there are people who've driven for years without studying the handbook. They just wouldn't be able to get a license without doing the written driving test.

How did we ever first learn to cook? We didn't have cookbooks way back when.

When I went to teachers college, studied teaching methods, education theory, and how to deal with students, did I know everything about teaching when they handed me my diploma?

The day I learned about teaching was the day I faced a Grade 9 classroom with thirty pairs of eyes looking at me expectantly. Did they know I was more scared than they were? Everything I'd learned in the books hadn't quite prepared me for that, or what I would encounter over the next eight years of teaching.

Can you see where I'm going here?

We learn by doing.

We can write by simply writing and not overthinking what we're writing while we're doing it.

As Stephen King states: *"You learn best by reading a lot and writing a lot, and the most valuable lessons of all are the ones you teach yourself."*

Since even Stephen King agrees with me, let's just...

4. STOP THINKING and START WRITING

What I'm going to ask you to do right now might seem kind of weird, given I've just been telling you to stop thinking. But I do want you to think about one more thing:

I want you to think about what happens when you're thinking.

Picture yourself this moment. What's happening inside your mind? You're reading my words. Thoughts are springing up in rapid succession ... uncensored, random thoughts:

Viga's a fruitcake!

I need to put my washing on.

I should put this book down or I'll get nothing done today.

Did I take the meat out to thaw for dinner?

Viga says write with abandonment.

You still need to know grammar, punctuation...

Was that the doorbell?

What time is it anyway?

Boy, I could use a coffee...

When we're going about our day doing this, that and every other thing, thoughts are tripping over themselves in our heads. We don't curb them. We don't censor them. We just let them flow. Occasionally, we get hung up on one train of thought but regardless, the thoughts keep moving along that track till something else springs to mind.

We don't worry about stopping any of those thoughts (most of us can't anyway) because we know no-one else is aware, at any given moment, what we are thinking. We don't worry that while our dearest friend is telling us about that pie she's making that we're thinking about that good looking young guy walking towards us!

Now what if we could just write like that?

Wouldn't it be wonderful if as we thought thoughts, they magically typed themselves onto the page.

"Oh, hold on", you say. "There's a lot of things I think that I wouldn't want anyone to know, let alone read."

Of course there are.

But who says you have to share any of those even after you stop writing? Until you decide to share them, the only person who sees them, reads them is YOU!

What's more, you have the right to go back later and change, edit, add, delete to your heart's content.

But the important thing is not to do any of that while you are writing!

Just write.

So, let me suggest that crazy idea again: Wouldn't it be wonderful if, as we thought thoughts, they magically typed themselves onto the page?

What's so wonderful about that?

It's what you would end up with:

The REAL you.

The one you hide away from everyone else most of the time.

If you could write that way now, this minute, and always, what would fall onto the pages, page after page would be the REAL you.

Barbara Turner Vesselago discovered the same thing when she

was struggling with the traditional approach. Her enormously popular creative writing book **"Writing Without a Parachute"** (highly recommended) confirms my thinking that this is the only process that helps us put the ME in MEmoir!

Barbara, myself and others call this type of writing "Freewriting". Others, like Stephen James, who wrote **"Story Trumps Structure",** describe it as "writing organically".

Whatever you want to call this type of writing, when you write without thinking about writing, letting the words fall freely from your heart and mind, you write YOURSELF onto that page: raw, naked, bare, uninhibited, uncensored.

That's YOU: a person just like the rest of us, far from perfect, vulnerable, and above all HONEST.

That's what happens when unbridled thoughts become words.

Okay. Since you now have to acknowledge that no-one but you knows what you're thinking unless you share it, are you ready to give "thoughts to words" a shot?

Let's try it. Remember, you don't have to share what you write in the next few minutes with anyone. It doesn't matter two hoots if what you write is garbage. All that matters is you write EVERYTHING that comes into your mind AS IT COMES.

Set this book aside now. Grab pen and paper, and start writing everything that comes up as if you just blew onto the white fluff of a dandelion, and are watching those puffy fluffs free falling through the air.

Come on. Let's go. Write down every thought now. Don't take your pen from the page for the next three minutes. Start writing...

****

Time's up! How did you go? How much did you write?

When we do this exercise in my workshop, some write an entire page, others only a few lines. I know those who write a page are writing all thoughts as they come to them.

Those with a few lines are either slow writers or are still censoring their thoughts and controlling their writing. They're still thinking *"Am I doing this right?" "Is this what she wants?"*

It's not about what I want. It's not about doing the right or wrong thing.

Those "slow" writers are back in that childhood classroom. They are not writing with abandonment.

But remember what I said five minutes ago? You don't have to share what you wrote with me or anyone.

Let's try it again. This time, I want you to watch a movie in your mind. The movie stars YOU on your first day in high school. What are you wearing? Who is nearby? What is the weather like? What sounds do you hear? What can you smell? Perfume? Hairspray? Is anyone talking? How are you feeling?

Now, as the movie plays, pick up your pen and start writing everything you see, hear and feel; every thought that enters your mind as it comes! No time limit. GO!

****

How did you make out this time? Was it easier? Did you write non-stop or did you do what I call 'stuttering on paper"? I hope you just wrote non-stop, freely, organically, with complete abandonment. Again, remember, you don't have to share any of that with anyone.

But now, go read what you wrote. Better yet, read it **OUT LOUD!**

What? Out loud? Why?

An amazing thing happens when you read what you've just written out loud. I'm doing it constantly as I write this book. To get myself back into writing mode day after day, I go back and read yesterday's chapter, OUT LOUD. As I do, I hear places where I could say it better. I hear spots where it's flowing beautifully and saying exactly what it should.

But most importantly, I can hear and feel if this sounds just like ME, the ME I hear chatting away to myself all the time in my head, the one I keep hidden from everyone else. The REAL ME.

Reading out loud to myself is another important part of the process of writing with abandonment; of putting ME into your MEmoir.

5 ADDRESSING THE INNER CRITIC

Isn't all this just journaling?

Yes, very similar. It comes from the same place and it's very much like journaling or writing a diary. It becomes memoir later...when you begin serious editing.

Did you use to keep a diary when you were younger?

Do you still keep one now?

If you do, you're miles ahead of everyone else who wants to write memoir. It's going to be so much easier to bring up those memories...both the good and bad.

Don't you wish now you hadn't stopped writing in your diary? For that matter, why did you stop? Did you just get too busy or were you afraid someone might find it and read it?

And if they had, what would they have found?

You know the answer: they would have found the real YOU before you started censoring all your thoughts, opinions, emotions; before you told yourself you shouldn't feel this way, think that way; before you let all the other voices you began listening to as you grew up tell you how you should think, feel, act or write; before all the critics took over your mind and became part of who you are right now, this minute, reading this book and thinking *"I can't possibly write a memoir this way!"*

I'm telling you *"Yes you can!"*

As I said earlier, I'm writing this book you're reading that way, jotting down my thoughts as they come into my head; not worrying about whether you think I'm nuts, or even whether any of this is helping you, or will result in you eventually writing your own memoir!

I can't afford to think about all that as I write. If I do, I'll hit a wall or get full blown writer's block, or worse yet, never finish this book!

If I stop to think, to re-read what I've just written in the past five minutes, I'll probably delete most of it! And there might be some really good ideas in there. So the time to delete it is not now, but later...much later. Perhaps tomorrow when I read it all back to myself, OUT LOUD, and find out what is and isn't working. Or perhaps I'll delete, edit, change when I've written the entire book. It doesn't matter when I do that part. All that matters NOW is that I keep writing!.

See, if I stop writing now, my inner critic, the one who was born from all the other voices I listened to as I was growing up and learning, will take over. When I am writing, I must not let that inner critic's voice guide my pen. If I do, the result might be what everyone else thinks and feels, and not what I think and feel. That just won't do.

This is a key part of writing with abandonment! And it's what you must do if you want to put yourself 100% into your MEmoir. The only voice that you, and others hear should be YOURS!

Let me share an experience I had about three years ago. I've always been hung up on my weight, and as I got older and really out of shape, there were times I broke down and cried over how my body had gone to pot with each passing decade. Menopause was a bitch!

One day, when I nearly puked on looking at myself in the mirror, I decided to blog my feelings instead of moping. I went online and began writing with abandonment just like I'm doing now. Before I hit publish, I re-read the post looking for grammar and spelling mistakes. I burst out laughing. It was hilariously funny and probably one of the best blog posts I've ever written. Apart from changing a sentence or two here and there, I published it just as it was. The result? So many followers responded to my post saying how much they loved it, how it had cracked them up, and how much they identified with what I was feeling.

A couple of years later, I ended up publishing it again, but this time as a little short story on **Smashwords**. Apart from giving it a title, nothing else had changed.

Imagine my delight when I received two 5-star reviews, both from men, who had this to say:

"Not what I expected to read about. A very unique kind of true-to-life short story (book). A very well deserved 5 star rating."

"Even as "a husband" I can relate to this wonderful little slice of life. Thanks for the great read, lol."

Those kinds of responses convinced me long before I actually wrote my first full memoir, that writing organically, "with abandonment" works; that when folks can hear ME, they respond to my words.

But my story about this article doesn't end there. Less than a year ago I decided to submit it to an anthology being published by a memoir teacher whose work I greatly admire. She responded quickly, said she loved my story, its humor and its "voice" and wanted to include it in the anthology. But now, would I mind expanding on it by adding those elements traditional books encourage: set the mood by describing my surroundings; add sensuous detail; use colors, textures to help readers visualize the scene more clearly etc., etc.

Gulp.

Well, I wanted my story in an anthology, didn't I. So, I went ahead, adding details like wearing a "flimsy pink see-through" nightie to bed...what a horrible visual that was...and sleeping on "blue satin sheets" soaked in perspiration...I don't have blue satin sheets...and wiping my sweaty face with a "candy-cane striped terrycloth" towel. If I really had one of those, I would have donated it to the Sally Ann ages ago.

I re-submitted the altered piece to her anthology. She loved it and included it. Cool!

She asked me if I could see how much better it was now. Looking at it from the traditional approach to writing, yes, it was better.

But did I like it? Nowhere as much as I did my original story. The voice wasn't mine. It was no longer ME.

I felt it had lost its snap, its vitality, its immediacy, its "relate-ability", because really, if I were sitting, chatting with you over coffee and telling you how the night sweats of menopause are driving me mad, would I also describe my "flimsy pink" nightie and "blue satin" bed sheets and that towel with candy cane stripes? Hardly!

I know as well as any writer that stories need settings, details to help readers visualize, anchor the scene. I just didn't feel that those details were what gave this story its punch, its humor, its power. Those were coming from my tone, my "voice". And that original voice spoke with complete abandonment and honesty.

You see, the altered story was Viga Boland, writer. The original story was Viga, human being. Far from perfect but oh, so real.

I may be wrong, and you have every right to disagree. But if I don't like what I write, what is the point of sharing with anyone else? Memoir is such a hugely personal genre of writing. Its strength lies in a story that captures your mind; emotions that make your heart race with sadness, anger, pain, or joy, all the emotions with which every other ordinary human being on this planet can identify.

If your memoir has all that other stuff: descriptive narrative passages, sensuous details and colorful words but lacks emotion, it has nothing worth reading, because YOU aren't in it.

As I recently read, and I wish I knew who said this, *"Unless you bring a beating heart to your message, it is dead."*

That initial approach I advocate so much, of writing freely, with abandonment, of throwing caution to the wind brings a beating heart to your message. Writing with abandonment releases YOUR voice and keeps the inner critic at bay. It puts ME into your MEmoir.

As I've said more than once already, there's plenty of time later to add, change, edit, delete. But get the real, raw stuff down first. Decide later how much of that you can comfortably share without your family disowning you, but don't worry about it as you write. Interestingly enough, you might be surprised how much you end up deciding to keep. But don't sabotage your writing by keeping all the "ME" locked up inside you in the first place!

If I may fall back yet again on Denis Ledoux's advice (he and I think alike)

"Perfectionism is not a virtue at this stage. Keep writing for volume. Quality will enter in later. Perfectionism is really a loss of faith in your work and in your vision. It pretends to be in your favor but it is really a prison. Avoid perfectionism."

So, on that note, let's say to heck with perfectionism, and to heck with that inner critic.

It's time to put this book aside again, to grab pen and paper and write. But this time I want you, with complete abandonment, to write a letter to that inner critic; that one inside you who keeps saying *"You can't do this."*

Take a second now to reflect on whose voices you're hearing every time you're about to try something different. It might be a parent's voice; a teacher's; or even that of your spouse. All those negative voices are now part of your own inner critic. And that inner critic is stopping you from moving on, from doing what you want to do: write a MEmoir.

Tell that inner critic where to go in no uncertain terms. Release your anger. Pick up that pen and start writing non-stop, freely, with complete abandon. Tell him/her to stop saying this is a waste of time. Tell him/her you're not going to listen to that negative voice any longer. Start writing now!

*****

I hope you completed the exercise above and wrote that letter to your inner critic. If you did, then you're serious about wanting to write memoir. If you didn't, then you just left a huge boulder in the middle of the path you were following in the hope you could write memoir, or write anything for that matter.

You need to trust me on this: it's nearly impossible to embark on anything in this life if you keep listening to those voices saying you can't do it. And the voice that is speaking the loudest at this point is your own.

So if you didn't write that letter to your inner critic, as suggested above, please stop reading now. Go back and re-read those last few paragraphs in the previous chapter. Then write that letter so you can move on.

6 WHY WRITE MEMOIR ANYWAY?

Now let's look further into this business of writing a memoir.

At this point you have every right to ask me *"Is that all there is to writing a memoir? You mean, all I have to do is pick up a pen and start writing whatever comes into my head?"*

Absolutely not!

What I've been doing with you up to this point is simply helping you free up your thinking, to help you get past so much of you've learned until now about writing so you can at least get started on your memoir. In doing so, I've been hoping to motivate you by making you believe you can do it.

But now, we do need to get into considering just for whom are you writing this book?

Before you jump in with the "noble", expected answers, be honest.

You write for yourself. We all do.

Don't want to take my word for it? Then listen to what the recognized expert, William Zinsser has to say in his book, **"On Writing Well"**:

"You are writing primarily to please yourself, and if you go about it with enjoyment you will also entertain the readers who are worth writing for."

Exactly: you need to enjoy, not be annoyed during the writing process.

Stephen King adds: *"When you write a story, you're telling yourself the story."*

Right on! We write to express ourselves. Maybe it's a bit narcissistic, but when one is having a conversation, whether on the phone or face to face, we run the risk of being interrupted, opposed, questioned.

When we write, provided we keep that inner critic at bay, we are free...free to express ourselves, to have our say on a subject we're passionate about, even if it's only a memory that's important to us.

Telling others what we want and how we truly feel is something society teaches us from childhood is not always acceptable, desirable or even wise! That's why journaling or keeping a diary is so therapeutic.

But now, since you're reading this book because you're thinking of writing a memoir, what do you plan to do with it when you're finished?

Who is your intended audience? Is it friends and family? Are you hoping to fulfill a lifelong dream of being a published author, of seeing your book in bookstores and libraries?

Many of us have that dream but are unable to realize it until we are retired and have time to write a book. That was certainly how it happened for me. And the good news is that it's never too late! How's that for encouragement?

Actually, when it comes to writing memoir, there are many who feel it is something that should wait until you're older, when you can bring a lifetime of experiences into your book. That way it's less likely to end up as just an overly emotional narrative of the trauma and drama that has happened, or is going on in your life right now. You may still need time to sort through all that before you write your memoir. Age does have a way of helping us see people, places and events more clearly, and from all sides, and not just our own.

So now, getting back to your intended audience: perhaps you've reached that stage in your life when you would like to leave a legacy of some kind for your children and grandchildren; perhaps your family and friends have always said you've got such great stories, you should write them down. That's very flattering and motivating, isn't it.

But when it comes to publishing your book and getting it into bookstores and libraries, you have to be realistic and ask yourself who, beyond my family and friends, will be interested in my memoir?

That depends 100% percent on the content. According to Jerry Waxler of **The Memoir Writers Network**,

"When we glance into the marshland of memory, we feel saddened by a past that is gone forever. To write a memoir, we set aside wistful nostalgia and approach our past with the attitude of curiosity and creativity. Page by page, we build paths that allow us to come and go more freely. Gradually we turn byways, mistakes, courage and survival into tales that entertain and educate others. By making our own past more accessible, we help others learn more about their possible future."

If that isn't a great reason to write memoir, I don't know what is.

There are two important words in what Jerry Waxler said above: *"entertain"* and *"educate"*. If the memoir you write doesn't entertain and educate, your readership may indeed be limited to your family and friends.

That, perhaps sadly for those who dream of seeing their books in stores, is one of the reasons memoirs aren't on publishers' "most wanted" lists. But the real truth is, unless you're a celebrity or famous, publishers know they won't be able to make some, if any money on publishing your memoir. After all, publishing is, first and foremost, a business.

Ah, I can hear you saying now *"Some of those books by celebrities are terrible, really badly written! I wouldn't spend my time or money buying those books!"*

But by the same token, would you shell out dollars to read the memoirs of someone you don't know from Adam? We all need a very compelling reason to pick up a memoir by someone we don't know.

I'm not being negative here, just realistic.

"Well then..." you ask, *"What memoirs might find a larger readership than my immediate friends and family?"*

Again, Jerry Waxler provides an answer. Those memoirs that give us

"... a window into human nature through the lens of story."

Those that enlighten us about how we think, or why we do what we do make for interesting reading.

Memoirs that explore psychological development, coming of age, family relationships and values, along with all the grief and hardship of just trying to survive, make for compelling reading. When readers feel, identify with the narrator's pain and desperation to find a solution to a problem, they pull for the narrator as they read. They keep turning pages hoping for a happy ending. And few things satisfy more than closing the book, knowing that in the end, the narrator came out on top.

Writing memoirs like that IS possible, if you remember to put the ME in your MEmoir by writing with abandonment in the first place!

"But, but," you say. *"I've had a wonderful life. Nothing horribly dramatic happened in my life."*

Well that's wonderful. So few of us can say that. And there are many out there who enjoy those stories that give us the "warm fuzzies". But when you write those, your words still need to make readers feel your joy and pleasure in just being alive, in experiencing all the places, people and things you've enjoyed, loved and from which you learned. You still have to put ME into your MEmoirs.

Here's one of the most important reasons for folks like you and me to write memoir: we can provide information people seek that is NOT available, even on the World Wide Web.

For instance, we can find everything currently known from a clinical and scientific point of view about medical concerns like cancer, Parkinson's Disease, ALS, dementia, just to name a few.

But how does it FEEL to have those diseases or live with, and care for someone who does?

We can get statistical and analytical information on Autism, ADHD, FASD, but how does it FEEL to have those disabilities or raise a child who does? What problems do parents face and where can they go for help? The person who writes a memoir on subjects like this, as my associate, Barbara Studham, did with **"Two Decades of Diapers"**, her often heart-wrenching memoir of single-handedly raising four grandchildren with FASD, has penned an invaluable resource! That first hand account can mean far more to the reader than all the information on the net.

The same can be said of those brave souls who write a memoir about social issues, e.g. overcoming drug or Alcohol addiction; transgenderism (**"I am Woman"** by Daliah Husu, or **"I Promised not to Tell"** by Cheryl B. Evans); child abuse (**"Where Children Run"**, Karen Emilson); cultural abuse (**"I am Malala"**); child sexual abuse (**"No Tears for my Father"**, Viga Boland); religious abuse, (**"Split"** by Mary Dispenza); domestic abuse (**"The Full Catastrophe"**, Karen Lee); abortion or the loss of a baby in a first pregnancy, or an adult child in your later years.

I have to stop a second here to point out that, with one exception, all those books above are written by non-famous writers who had an important story to share. Traditional publishers may have passed on their books. I am personally grateful that they believed in the value of their stories enough to self-publish. I've learned so much from each of them.

These, and others issues like them, are such incredibly sensitive, often hidden or denied subjects. There's tons of information on the Internet about all of them, but all that information will not move us, or mean as much to us as a first hand account by someone who's lived through these true life situations.

That, for me, is why writing memoir matters. These are stories for everyday people living with what we have lived with, who want help beyond the facts and figures and need the consolation of knowing they are not alone. What an important and worthwhile service we memoirists can provide!

7 MEMOIR? BIOGRAPHY?
AUTOBIOGRAPHY?

Which one do you want to write? Do you know the difference between them? There really is a difference.

Here's what they have in common: all three genres are true stories about real people, places and events, and accuracy matters.

BIOGRAPHIES are usually written by someone about someone else's life and achievements. They are written in the third person (he, she, as opposed to I, we) and generally cover several decades in that person's life, often their entire life. Facts, figures, events take precedence over feelings and emotions. Biographies are usually about the rich, the famous, the movers, the shakers or those whose good works have impacted lives. Think Mother Theresa, Martin Luther King.

AUTOBIOGRAPHIES are generally self-written, again by persons well known in any industry or walk of life. But those busy people may commission others to write their life stories for them. In the respect that they are about somebody famous, and cover almost an entire lifetime, they are similar to biographies. Autobiographies are written in the first person (I, we) and may contain more emotion and feelings than a biography would.

MEMOIRS, like autobiography are always written in first person. Like both the other genres, they share facts, figures and events but there is a much greater focus on the psychology and emotions of the narrator and all the people involved in the narrator's life. Memoirs draw the reader's attention to the whys, hows, and wherefores more so than the whats.

One primary difference with memoir is the time span covered: generally no more than one or two decades in a person's life. The other big difference is memoir usually presents one critical, eventually life-changing situation, and shows how the narrator faced that situation and dealt with it. Memoirs are almost always far more personal, friendly, even conversational. They invite the reader inside the narrator's mind and heart, and if written well, the memoir shouts *"This is me without my mask."*

So now, which of the three do you want to write?

By the way, you can write a biography or even an autobiography of your non-famous but amazing, adventurous grandfather, or your beloved grandmother. You can even bring in their feelings and emotions. But it's not exactly a "memoir".

You can also write your own autobiography, even if you're not rich or famous and have never faced a life changing situation. In that case you're more likely to be focused on what you've seen, done and achieved and how various situations impacted you. You may state how you felt at the time, but most likely, you won't go too deeply into the nitty-gritty. This then becomes a bit like a series of vignettes, or what I call "mini-memoirs".

For instance, you might share what Christmas or Thanksgiving traditions you follow; how you felt when you landed your first job and some of the things that went wrong or right; what it was like leaving home and moving into your own apartment; or you could tell of the events leading up to and including the birth of your first child. These are all stories to which most of us can relate and many enjoy reading.

So now after all that, do you know which one you want to write? I hope so because that's all I'm going to say about it, except to suggest that right now, once again, you set this book aside and take 5, maybe 10 minutes to jot down all the thoughts tumbling through your mind.

By doing that right now, you are sorting through what you really want to write. Again, remember the most important rule here: write with abandon. Don't stop to think. Just jot everything down as it comes. When you're finished, read it back to yourself, OUT LOUD. You may find something jumps out at you. Let's hope so, because that something might be what you will ultimately write and didn't realize before now: memoir, autobiography or biography.

GO!

8 SUMMONING UP AND ORGANIZING YOUR MEMORIES

I don't know how old you are, but I was 65 when I started my first memoir, **"No Tears for my Father"**. That's a lot of times, places and events I needed to dredge up, not to mention the emotions I experienced during the twenty years between ages 11 - 24 on which I intended to focus. Like, all of that took place 40 - 50 years ago!

Even with the sequel **"Learning to Love Myself"**, (which was actually more of an autobiography since it covered ages 24 to the present), it was hard. It covered forty years of times, places, events and emotions. Furthermore, while it was a continuation of the first memoir, its focus wasn't just one situation I had to deal with, but many of them.

So what does one do to summon up all those memories, let alone organize them?

Well one of the best suggestions I came across, and this works really well for those longer biographies and autobiographies, is to create TIMELINES.

This is how you do it. Grab a sheet of paper and divide it into vertical columns. At the top of each, write 0 - 9, 10 - 19, 20 - 29, 30 - 39 and so on and so on, depending on how old you are. Those are DECADES in your life.

After you've drawn the columns (the easy part), start thinking back, back to those decades. What were you doing, say, between 10 - 19? Who were your friends? How did you spend your time? What did you enjoy most? What hobbies did you have?

Any traumatic events occur during that time? If so, how did you feel? Perhaps you moved and had to change schools? How hard was that? Maybe dad lost his job. How did mom take it? Did you get engaged? Call off the wedding? Get married? Lose your best friend? Change jobs?

Get the idea?

Start filling in the timeline in each column with as many events as you can remember. Dig out old photos. Look through them. Who's in that picture? What did that person mean to you? Was that someone special? Your first love perhaps. How did you feel? Did you two have a favorite song? Can you remember it? What was happening in the world at that time? Any important events?

Jot down everything you can think of. All of it. Every thought. And add how you FELT as each event took place, e.g. *"Beloved pet hit by car...distraught"*.

Jot with abandon! DON'T censure! Nothing is too trivial. That memory that just flashed across your mind might seem insignificant just now. But it might remind you of something important the next time you glance at that decade's timeline. So leave it in. No scratching out.

To make the best use of that decades timeline sheet, Keep it handy to where you are writing. Perhaps you won't get a chance to write for several days. The best way to get the flow running again is to re-read your last couple of chapters. As you do, other events, feelings might surface. It might be an event that didn't occur in that chapter, but later on. Memories have a way of prompting other memories once you get started. So, immediately add that memory to that timeline "for later". If you don't, guaranteed you'll forget it when you get to that part.

And as you go about your day, if something occurs to you i.e. you suddenly remember an event, a moment...a favorite song comes on the radio...for heaven's sake drop what you're doing (unless you're holding your grandchild or reaching for a pot on the stove) and grab that sheet. Add that memory or thought to it immediately. Memories are such fleeting things and nothing flees faster than thoughts!

What other ways can you summon up memories?

Go online and research world events that were occurring during those decades. A very helpful site for that is *www.onthisday.com*

When I was writing my memoir, **"The Ladies of Loretto"**, (a fun look at my four years in a Catholic girls high school during the early sixties), I suddenly remembered being in Grade 11 the day President Kennedy was assassinated. Like 911 so many years later, the event affected me deeply. I knew others felt likewise. Why not bring into my memoir the reactions of the students and teachers in the classroom when the news broke?

Of course I wrote that scene into the story and when I'd finished, I thought of checking that website above to see what else was happening in the world over those four years. Talk about great memory joggers! I found events, people, places I might never have thought of otherwise, e.g. the "Twist" being declared sinful by the Catholic Church; the Beatles exploding on the music scene. By the time I'd finished writing the book, I knew that as others read the **"The Ladies of Loretto"**, they too would stop to think *"What was I doing that day?"* Or chuckle to themselves saying *"I remember that!"*

Adding major events this way makes your memoir relevant to your readers. But one caution here: avoid the temptation to start quoting too much recorded data about such events.

Doing so can slow your story down. While a memoir can and should "educate", remember the focus is feelings, not things. Bogging your memoir down with details readers can find online or in history books will take away from the other hugely important reason why people read: entertainment. And memoir, being the "friendliest", most informal and personal format of the three styles (biography, autobiography, memoir) needs to entertain.

As James Scott Bell, says in his book, **"How to make a living as a writer"**:

"People who read want one of two things: knowledge or entertainment. When you can give them both, so much the better. Learn to tell the story readers won't want to put down. For example, if you're a novelist, your first job is to entertain...if the reader doesn't read your book it doesn't matter what your message is."

Before you jump on me and say *"But I thought you were talking about writing memoirs, not novels,"* let me just tell you this: the more your memoir reads like a novel, the more readers will enjoy it! After all, what is memoir if not a story? You can quote me on that!

I'll have more to say about that later, but, for now, just keep in mind that too much data, too many facts, too many details will weigh your memoir down like an overloaded wagon stuck in the mud. Resist the urge!

Okay. Time for a break, and time for you to keep practising writing with abandonment. I know I've jolted a ton of thoughts and memories with everything I've just said. So go ahead. Set this book aside and jot down what you're remembering, thinking, feeling, right this minute.

For the next 5 minutes start writing, non-stop. GO!.

9 NUTS AND BOLTS

Okay. We're about to move into the heavier stuff now but in the lightest way I can do it. There are so many books out there that teach the "craft of writing". Feel free to invest in as many as you can afford. Most will remind you of everything you learned in Composition and Literature classes back in high school.

Forgive me for smiling at that thought. But if I start throwing all those school day "must-haves" at you, as I did in my first series of workshops, I know what's going to happen: your eyes will glaze over; you'll yawn; self-doubt will creep in; the inner critic will take over and you'll set this book aside to make yourself coffee, go take a walk or put on that load of washing you should be doing instead of dreaming about writing a book.

That's the last thing I want when my primary purpose for this book is to motivate you to write a memoir, to make you believe you can do it.

So I'm going to keep doing this my way, and just in case you're wondering, yes, I'm still writing this book organically, with abandon, just as the words fall onto the page, because that's really the only way I can relax when writing. I like to enjoy what I'm doing.

Okay, let's get back to those nuts and bolts with this excerpt from my second memoir, **"Learning to Love Myself"**, but with a little bit of background first. The scene below took place while we were on our honeymoon. We'd been camping across Canada for a week. We were both exhausted from all the hours on the road. Here's what happened:

I heard something crunch under my bottom as I slid back into the car.

"Where the heck are my sunglasses?" John asked.

Oh no. Don't tell me. I re-opened my door and jumped back out of

36

the car. John's sunglasses lay broken on my seat. One of the hinges had snapped and the frame was totally bent. He spotted them the same time I did.

"Oh shit! You sat on my sunglasses? They're the only pair I have with me. How am I supposed to drive with that sun setting in front of us? Didn't you see them?" I winced as the flat of his palm came down hard on the steering wheel.

Tears sprung to my eyes. Why was this my fault?

Earlier, he'd nearly lost control of the car when he'd heard a plane overhead and was trying to pull over to get yet another damn photo, one of the hundreds already taken on this trip. He'd pulled up hard. I'd hopped out quickly, happy to stretch my legs, and he'd thrown his precious sunglasses onto my seat as he'd reached over the back for his camera. Was I supposed to see everything?

"How is this my fault?" I asked. "I didn't put the sunglasses there!" As brave as I sounded, inwardly I was cringing. I'd never spoken in my defence when my father was angry at me, yet somehow I'd found the courage to defend myself now. Doing this was so out of character it scared me.

John wouldn't be pacified. "How couldn't you see them when you were getting back in the car?"

"Oh for Pete's sake," I yelled in frustration, "they're just a pair of bloody sunglasses. You can pick up another pair in the next town we come to."

Now, why have I shared this excerpt? Because it exemplifies some of the key "nuts and bolts" that novelists use, but we memoir writers need to use as well: DIALOGUE; SHOWING INSTEAD OF TELLING; presenting CONFLICT and increasing TENSION, not just in the characters, but also in the readers.

Here we have young newlyweds, deeply in love, engaged in one of the many arguments they will have over their married lives. We are finding out what they are like through the exchange of dialogue, and through their actions e.g. *"I winced as the flat of his palm came down hard on the steering wheel."*

No loaded descriptions, or long narratives told or seen only though the eyes of the narrator. Instead, we learn about the characters through the actions and words of both speakers. As they argue, conflict increases in the scene, raising tension in the reader who wonders what will happen next.

This tension of wondering what will happen next matters just as much in memoir as it does in fiction. Why? Because all said and done, memoir writing is telling a story and just like fiction, to be enjoyed, it must capture and hold reader interest.

According to popular novelist and speaker, Stephen James, stories must do much more than tell us what happened: they have to tell us WHAT WENT WRONG, or as in the excerpt above, how it went wrong and got worse.

In his fabulous book, **"Story Trumps Structure"**, (highly recommended) Stephen James illustrates this need by sharing a tale from his days of visiting elementary schools. Do you remember when you returned to classes each September and the first thing you were told to write in English composition class was *"How I spent my summer"*? Groan. Every year. Same composition. Only the events changed as you grew older. Boring!

So, when Stephen visited this one class, instead of getting students to tell the class what they did over the summer holidays, he asked them to tell about something that went wrong. One little fellow put up his hand and told this delightful story:

"My cousin came over to my house, and we were having a contest to see who could jump the farthest off my bunk bed."

"What happened?" I asked.

"He went first and got pretty far, and I said, 'I can get farther than that!'"

The boy was a natural storyteller, and by then everyone in the class was leaning forward, waiting to hear how things played out.

38

"Well, what went wrong?"

"I backed up to the wall to get a running start...and I jumped off the bed...and the ceiling fan was on. I got my head stuck in the ceiling fan, and it threw me against the wall—but I got farther!"

The class cracked up.

(Taken from Story Trumps Structure (Writers Digest Books, 2014) by Steven James, used by permission)

Wonderful isn't it? And that came out of the mouth of a fourth grader! Stephen James calls the idea behind the importance of telling the reader what went wrong, **'The Ceiling Fan Principle'**.

I say, keep that 'Ceiling Fan Principle' working throughout your memoir (or memoirs if you are writing a collection of stories) and you will end up with a book others want to read and tell their friends about!

I'm reading and reviewing one like that just now. It's called **"Far and Away"** by Russell Sunshine. (No kidding! That's his real name). It's a delightful collection of "true tales from an international life". Russell Sunshine shares stories from his travels around the world, beginning with his childhood. Now a book like this could easily turn into a travelogue full of geographic and cultural information...you know, all those facts we can find for ourselves on the net.

But Russell Sunshine knows better than to bore us that way. Something goes wrong in just about every short tale, keeping us keen to turn pages to see what happens in the next story. I wonder if Russell had read or heard Stephen James 'Ceiling Fan Principle' when he wrote his memoirs! Maybe. Or maybe, like that fourth grader, Russell is just a natural born story teller.

Are you?

Of course you are! If you can talk, you can tell a story! Most of us tell stories, (some of them not even true!) all the time.

But, when it comes to writing a novel or a MEmoir, one that will rivet readers, a story must be

"...about how the things that happen affect someone in pursuit of a difficult goal, and how that person changes internally as a result." (Lisa Cron, **"Story Genius")**

Basso Canto, who reviewed Lisa Cron's book, **"Story Genius"**, says

"No matter how beautiful the prose, if it doesn't relate to the protagonist's struggle, the story falls flat."

It's that "Ceiling Fan Principle" whirring again, reminding the story-teller that ***"Unless you bring a beating heart to your message, it is dead."***

10 IF YOU CAN TALK, AND MAKE US HEAR OTHERS TALK, YOU CAN WRITE DIALOGUE.

Dialogue! That word. Ugh!

The minute I mention using dialogue in my workshops, I see panic in the faces around the table. They look like I must have when my Grade 6 teacher told us we had to enter the upcoming public speaking competition. I'm sure a look akin to a fear of death itself was written all over my face. That's how my workshop participants look as they think:

I don't know how to use quotation marks!

Do I write "he said", "she said" each time someone speaks?

I'll need a thesaurus to keep replacing "said".

Couldn't I just narrate what was said during the conversation. It'd be so much easier...

Easier, yes. And so much more boring too. Not to mention how much ongoing narration slows down the action in both the story and the reader. Eyes blur looking at all those solid blocks of text on the page, page after page.

But inject some dialogue and suddenly, the reader is zipping along, caught up in the moment. Characters come alive and so does the reader. It's like watching a movie or a sit-com: people are talking or screaming at each other across a room. We see them; hear them; feel them.

Today, more than ever, we live in a highly visual world, thanks to modern technology and media. We are awash in high definition graphics, full color TV, social media selfies, YouTube and Snapchat. We chase Pokemons down our streets and off cliff edges following the little critters on cell-phones. Movies explode with special effects.

And here we sit trying to compete with all those visual inputs with only words. What a job we have! We can't let our stories become documentaries delivered by Walter Cronkite.

Memoirs are about real people. They are far more memorable if we can make them come alive as they do on a movie screen.

Dialogue makes characters come alive on the page.

Make them TALK...but not through a narrator!

Make them talk to each other!

Noted authority on writing, Elmore Leonard, in his often quoted **"10 Rules of Writing"** uses this quote from a John Steinbeck novel to illustrate how important it is for characters in a story to speak for themselves and not through a narrator. He points out that in Steinbeck's book, one of the characters says:

"I like a lot of talk in a book and I don't like to have nobody tell me what the guy that's talking looks like. I want to figure out what he looks like from the way he talks."

Exactly right!

Help your reader watch scenes in the lives of real people by using dialogue, as I did in that honeymoon scene about the broken sunglasses. Sure, I could have narrated it. But if I had, it would have lost so much of its immediacy, its urgency, its "life".

So, you ask, how does one write that dialogue? Well in the case of mine above, just the same way I've been writing this book and am suggesting you write yours...at least initially. Write the dialogue freely, organically, just as it comes up from your memory, and right onto the page.

Picture the scene. Write the script. Let's try it now.

For the next few moments relive an argument you had with your husband or partner. Can you see yourselves? Hear yourselves? If nothing comes up (you mean you've never argued? You Fibber!) how about an argument with your son or daughter? A co-worker.

A traffic cop. Your doctor. Anyone.

Got one now? Okay. Grab a pen and paper. Close your eyes.

Now listen to the voices. Hear them? Yours? Theirs? Write those voices onto the page as you hear them speak. Don't censor. Don't change words. Write exactly what you hear them saying as the words come up. Don't stop, scratch out and say, *"No, it wasn't like that."* Exact words don't matter.

Forget about "he said", "she said". Just write!

Done?

Now, read what you've written. It might be a little hard to read right now if you didn't put each speaker's words on a different line. That's OK. you can do that later. All that mattered in this exercise was getting out the words each said.

Now read it again as if each speaker were on a different line, but this time, read it OUT LOUD!

You **must** read dialogue you've written **out loud**. We don't speak silently except in our heads, right? The only way to know if the dialogue is flowing naturally, if the words sound like the speaker's real voice, is to read the dialogue out loud. Can you hear your husband's or child's voice or does it sound like you saying what they said?

If the latter, do the exercise again using a different argument. (I hope you're normal and have had more than one argument in your life!)

Now, read that second one OUT LOUD. Is it any better? If you're not sure, get someone else to read it to you out loud.

If you sound like you, and the other person sounds like himself/herself, then you've succeeded.

Need more confirmation you've really captured another's voice? Ask someone who knows the other person very well to silently read that part containing the dialogue. If they can "hear" that person's voice saying the words as they read to themselves, you've nailed it.

I didn't even think of asking anyone in my family to do that for me when I was writing my memoirs. It was only later, when my younger daughter who was reading my second book, **"Learning to Love Myself"** put it down, turned to me and said:

"Oh my God, mom, Can I ever hear Pop's voice! That's exactly how he used to yell and intimidate everyone! He scared me stupid!"

That's when it occurred to me this was an ideal way to be sure what I thought sounded like someone actually did.

You know, all of this isn't really that hard if we just write, instead of trying so hard to be writers.

STOP TRYING TO BE A WRITER! JUST WRITE!

If using caps make it seem like I'm shouting, I am. I need to make my point: Just write. You CAN do this.

Put on your writers' and editors' hats AFTER you've written the stories. But for now, as I've said all along, just write!

If you can talk, you can write!

Now, before I forget: about that business of using "he said, she said" and a different line for each speaker as they speak...

YES! You do need to put each speaker's new words on a separate line. That way you clue the reader in, even without using "he said, she said" that each of them is responding to the previous speaker's words e.g.

Mary jumped up from the cafe table to hug Joan. They hadn't seen each other in five years.

"Joan! So happy to see you again. It's been ages."

"Too long Mary."

Joan adjusted the hat that Mary had nearly knocked off her head in her excitement.

Mary indicated the wrought-iron chair opposite her. "Sit. Sit! So tell me everything that's been happening. Are you still married to Stephen?"

Joan smiled, but her eyes told Mary something her reply didn't: "Yes, we're still together".

Notice the lack of "she saids" in the above piece. The writer is acting like a director and moving the reader's eyes from one woman to another as if there was a camera filming the scene. That's the beauty of envisioning dialogue between two people as if it were a scene in a movie while you are actually writing it.

Try it every time you decide to add dialogue. Picture the scene; listen to the people talking; write what they are saying as they say it. Use a different line for each new line of speech by a different speaker. Add some details to set the scene in time and place before the dialogue occurs. Add little details about the setting as you move along, eg. the wrought-iron chair.

Oh, by the way, unless you're thinking I'm suggesting you never use "he said, she said", I'm not. There are times you have to do that so the readers don't lose their way in a longer conversation. But as Stephen King advises in his memoir on writing, don't agonize over using anything more than "said". Said is enough.

11 SHOW, DON'T TELL!

Along with dialogue, "show don't tell" is the other command that makes workshop participants' faces turn pale, and active minds go blank. Their eyes downcast, folks start sinking lower in their seats, almost sliding under the table in the hope I won't ask them if they know the difference.

Why? What's the big deal?

Well, in the simplest terms, it's writing *"Johnny charged down the street"* instead of *"Johnny ran down the street"*. Or *"Sandy gunned the car as if someone was shooting at it"* instead of *"Sandy drove down the road in a huge hurry"*.

"Oh, that's easy," you say. *"I'll just grab the Thesaurus when I'm editing."*

Good idea. But "Show, don't Tell" is about more than finding better suited adjectives for bland ones, or using similes and metaphors.

The reason for "Show, don't tell" is the same as the reason for using dialogue. It has to do with that "movie mind" world we live in today. Watching things happen is more powerful than being told what happened.

Just about every day, most of us meet with, or interact with others. We get to know them, love them or hate them based on what they say and DO.

So, when we write memoir, we need to SHOW the reader what those people are DOING instead of just TELLING what they are doing. If our mind is the only one our readers hear and see, then the reader gets a skewed image of the other characters: they get only the narrator's opinion of them. As I see it, that's the danger behind those memoirs that rely too much on narration and reflection. Everything is one-sided, unless you are very skilled as is my associate, Toni Pacini, in her book **"Alabama Blue"**:

The real sadness that day, and the source of my sorrowful memory wasn't solely because a child had died. The real horror came from what I heard the grownups say only minutes after the dead boy's tiny, golden brown body, glistening with beads of water catching the day's sunlight, was removed from the lake. The grown-ups laughed, some genuine, some nervous and uncertain, but they laughed.

One man said, "No big loss; one less nigger to put up with."

In response a big, red-faced man laughed with a crude snort, and said, "Hell, I didn't even know snakes liked dark meat."

I learned that day that not all snakes are belly crawlers. The two-legged ones can sometimes be meaner than the ones who slither and hiss.

©Toni Pacini, Alabama Blue. Reprinted with permission

That last line is just so powerful, don't you agree?

It's far better, and more effective, if we let the other people in our story speak for themselves and SHOW us, not just through their spoken words, but through their actions what they are really like. Indeed, Toni has done that above. By DOING SO, we allow our readers to form their own opinions of these other people in our stories. We are being less subjective, less biased.

Need some more examples? Try these:

"Nathan loved playing his guitar."

The narrator is telling us what Nathan likes to do. But below, the narrator lets Nathan's own actions show us how much he loves playing his guitar:

"When I first got together with Nathan, I'd come out of the shower to find him sound asleep on his back on the bed, his arms cradling the guitar and his fingers still glued to the strings. I realized then my only real competition was that guitar."

Here's another:

"My dad was a carpenter, complete with the tools of his trade." (Telling)

"Dad left the house each morning with his saw and hammer dangling from his belt. His left thumbnail was black. Every night when he returned from a job, mom lovingly brushed a fine coating of sawdust from his cheeks and wood chips out of his hair."

What a clearer picture we have now of dad when the narrator SHOWED us how he earned a living rather than merely telling us! And what did we glean about the relationship between mom and dad, just through mom's actions?

That's the power of showing, not telling. Yes, it takes more effort and it uses more words.

That last sentence I wrote prompted an alarm to go off in my head. Here's what the alarm suggested I should tell you: once you've written your entire memoir freely, organically and with abandon and it's time to edit, tighten, chop, add...all the really hard part of writing...don't start getting carried away "showing not telling" every time you want to reveal a bit more about a character.

It's really okay to leave some straight telling in there e.g. *"Mom was really nervous about my decision to move out on my own".* Sure, you can draw us a much stronger picture of mom's nervousness by showing her smoking several cigarettes in a row, chewing her nails while thinking about what she's just been told, etc. But if you do that all the time, everywhere throughout your memoir, it can become a bit too much. Not to mention that it'll increase he word and page count big time!

In a blot post about "Show don't Tell at ***http://www.dailywritingtips.com,*** the writers advise using a proper balance of showing and telling to make your writing more interesting and effective. They give just 4 rules:

1. Use Dialogue
2. Use Sensory Language (ie.. appeal to the 5 senses)
3. Be descriptive (adjectives, adverbs...use adverbs sparingly according to Stephen King and other gurus of writing)

4. Be specific, not vague e.g. "Mary was nice". "Nice" is one of the vaguest, most overused adjectives around! How/why was Mary "nice"?

I could go on and on about how to edit your book beyond what's been suggested in this chapter. But again, getting too "teacherish" (did I just coin a new word?) bores me and might bore you. Don't want that to happen.

So let me suggest a book I've just stumbled across that will help you more. It's a light read as well. Check out **"Fiction-Writing Modes: Eleven Essential Tools for Bringing Your Story to Life"** by Mike Klaasen at ***https://www.mikeklaassen.com.*** It's one of the handiest "quick-refs" I've found.

12 PUTTING "ME" INTO YOUR MEMOIR

Now I know the experts on memoir writing who may read this book are going to ask at this point:

"Is that all you're going to tell your readers about how to write memoir? Do you really think that they can go write a memoir now based on what you've given them?"

My honest answer to that has to be: *"I don't know!"*

But then how do they know their readers, or the folks in their workshops, are any better equipped...or perhaps I should say "likely"...to go out and write that very personal book known as memoir?

They don't...no more than I do.

Because once you shut this book, or leave a workshop, what happens after that is completely up to you.

As I said in my introduction to this book, my primary purpose in writing it was to motivate you; to encourage you; to make you believe you can write your memoir(s) and to help you see that it's not as hard as perhaps you have been telling yourself. Only YOU can tell me if I have achieved that goal.

But this I do know: you CAN do it

IF you write with abandonment

IF you disregard everything you learned in school about how to write and just write

IF you silence the voice(s) of that inner critic

IF you can visualize events, conversations, and people's actions as you would scenes in a movie or TV show

IF you can hear, and really listen, to what the people in your stories are saying as they talk to you and others, then write what they say organically, freely, as you hear it

IF you can leave all the editing, changing, adding, deleting, improving until you finish writing your memoir.

If you can do all that, you will also achieve what is implied in this book's title: you will have put ME into your MEmoir.

And after all, what is a memoir without ME? That is, without YOU?

But even if you do all the "IF's" above, you can still come up short on "ME" content...that is, "the real you" that I promised would emerge when you write organically.

What? Why? How?

That might happen when you reach the editing stage. During editing, unless you can be totally objective (as a professional editor who doesn't know you or your family would be) you might start listening again to those inner critics...the ones who tell you not to share those innermost thoughts, those very private family secrets; the ones who make you start worrying about who might be hurt or who might even sue you. I have seen talented memoirists with brilliant stories throw out months of work after re-reading all they'd written for fear of backlash.

How can you avoid having that happen to you? By informing the family of your plans and reasons for your memoir before you begin writing. Remember, memoir is truth, as closely as you remember it. And also keep in mind that no two people, even witnessing the same event, see it the same way. Each of us responds differently to the same stimuli because we are unique. And each of us REMEMBERS events based on our individual responses to them.

So arguments will arise regarding your version of the truth. Expect them. But also remember this is YOUR memoir, not theirs.

If you start editing out all the details of events in your life as YOU experienced and responded to them emotionally, you will edit the ME out of your MEmoir!

As C.S Larkin, author of **"Shoot your Novel"**, says:

"Readers want to be immersed in story and character, and you can't achieve that by holding them at arm's length—or relegating them to standing a hundred yards away." (C.S. Larkin, "Shoot Your Novel")

And don't ever forget what I said way, way back about memoir:

"Unless you bring a beating heart to your message, it is dead".

13 WRITING IS THE EASY PART: DON'T MAKE IT HARD. EDITING, ON THE OTHER HAND...

I don't want to spend forever on editing as there's already a wealth of information (both in books and online) about how to edit. Much of that information is written by famous writers and teachers far more skilled than I am. So why re-invent the wheel and risk demotivating you in the process?

But I do have one cardinal rule about editing, and you already know what it is:

DON'T EDIT WHILE YOU ARE WRITING!

Don't do anything that might disrupt the creative flow of thoughts to words.

Let me reassure you immediately that I am far from alone in my thinking on this! One of the best books I've ever read on memoir writing is by a famous writer...and the last person in the world I expected to study when researching how to write memoir: Stephen King. Yes, Stephen King.

I wasn't even a fan of his genre. But when I came across an interview with Stephen King in ***Rolling Stone***, where King was talking about his latest book (at that time), **"Revival"**, I became curious about both the book and Stephen King. In that interview, he indicated there were memoir aspects to the story he told in "Revival". I ended up purchasing not only "Revival" but also Stephen King's book: **"On Writing: A Memoir Of The Craft"**

That was one of the best investments in my writing that I ever made. I couldn't put down that book! King blew me away, not just with his knowledge, but with his wonderfully open, uncluttered, conversational style of writing. For me, it validated my own approach to writing, which as you know, if you've read this far, is pretty much straight off the cuff. Person to person. Me to you. I write it as I think it. Or more accurately, as it falls onto the page.

As I read how Stephen King actually writes, my heart rate increased. I was excited. His first rule of writing? The same as mine:

"GET IT OUT! Write a first draft and don't stop to edit your writing. Just write!"

His reasons for saying that? The same as the ones I gave you in the previous chapter and earlier in the book: that's the only way to muzzle that inner critic. It frees YOUR voice.

Stephen King? You rock! You just made me a fan for life.

What other ideas of mine on writing does Mr. King support? *"Don't obsess over perfect grammar"*.

Right on again. At least, don't obsess while you're writing, creating. Just let it flow.

After reading Stephen King's book, and there's more I want to share with you shortly, I researched the thoughts of many eminent gurus on this "Don't edit, just write" approach of mine. I found lots of support, including these:

"If it sounds like writing, rewrite it. Or, if proper usage gets in the way, it may have to go. I can't allow what we learned in English composition to disrupt the sound and rhythm of the narrative." © Elmore Leonard, "Elmore Leonard's 10 Rules of Writing"

"I do not over-intellectualize the writing process. I try to keep it simple. Tell the damn story!" (Tom Clancy, Writer's Digest)

"One thing that helps is to give myself permission to write badly. I tell myself I'm going to do my 5 or 10 pages no matter what, and that I can always tear them up the following morning if I want." (Lawrence Block, Writers Digest)

And I love this one I used some time ago in my online memoir writing magazine, **MEMOIRABILIA**, by Denis Ledoux of ***The Memoir Network***:

"Being stuck, remaining too long, in the editor/critic mode is not

good for your writing. When you are mired in the editor/critic function, you write, you re-write and re-write so as to "get it perfect." The problem is that no one can ever gets it perfect—no one."

Touche, Denis!

But sooner or later, we have to edit what we let flow organically, freely, with total abandonment onto those pages. As Patricia Fuller who wrote **"Editor Pet Peeves and how to avoid them"** once said:

"Writing without revising is the literary equivalent of waltzing gaily out of the house in your underwear."

Great analogy Patricia. In fact, when it comes to memoir writing, waltzing out of the house in your underwear applies to more than just editing. When I was publishing my magazine, **Memoirabilia**, I coined the phrase **"Memoir is a Selfie in Words"**. Think about that...but please don't chicken out equating memoir to putting a photo of you in your birthday suit on Facebook.

Moving right along, how soon after you finish writing should you begin editing? Well, if you're Stephen King, you throw the manuscript in a drawer and forget about it for six weeks or even longer! Given how prolific the man is, that method obviously hasn't hurt his sales. But when he begins editing, he goes at it with the same gusto that he writes. King's famous words on editing? *"To write is human; to edit is divine"*.

We less experienced writers would probably never regard editing as "divine". To be honest, I hate it: it's darn hard work, and many of us would rather give that job to someone else. In fact, we should. I didn't do it with my first book. Big mistake. You see, I use my iPad, not paper and pen to write. Well, you know what auto-correct is like? Even though I read and re-read my memoir, corrected, chopped and deleted before sending it to print, I still missed things. To my horror and embarrassment, two hundred books later, folks were catching auto-correct's incorrections. Groan.

So that's just one good reason to have professional proofreaders and editors instead of doing it yourself. The other reason has to do with being objective. It's super hard to be objective when it comes to our own creations. Just look what Stephen King has to say about that part of editing:

"When your story is ready to re-write, cut it to the bone. Get rid of every ounce of excess fat. This is going to hurt: revising a story down to the bare essentials is always a little like murdering children but it must be done."

Ouch! But again, Stephen King is right. He also follows Elmore Leonard's 10 Rules of Writing. Elmore says this when it comes to editing;

"Leave out the boring parts...the part readers tend to skip. Think of what you skip reading a novel: thick paragraphs of prose you can see have too many words in them."

Do you skip those? I sure do.

And never forget what Elmore Leonard quoted from that John Steinbeck novel about using dialogue:

"I like a lot of talk in a book and I don't like to have nobody tell me what the guy that's talking looks like. I want to figure out what he looks like from the way he talks."

So do I. And that's why I'm a huge fan of using dialogue instead of narrative in your memoir. Not only is it much more effective at revealing character, but it nips boredom in the bud and speeds up the pace of your memoir.

Bottom line? When you're editing, check to see if you have long paragraphs that describe the characters in your stories instead of letting us learn about those characters through what they say and do. As Leonard says:

"Don't go into great detail describing places and things, unless you're Margaret Atwood and can paint scenes with language. You don't want descriptions that bring the action, the flow of the story, to a standstill."

By the way, both Stephen King and Elmore Leonard are big on chopping out adverbs. Most newer writers use them everywhere. Until I read King's book, I wasn't aware of just how often I was using adverbs. Boy, am I aware of it now.

Ditto exclamation marks. Again, I never noticed it in my first memoir but when I look back over it, I cringe...more than just a little. If you want to know why Leonard and King feel that way, go get yourself a copy of Stephen King's book, **"On Writing: A Memoir Of The Craft"**.

And while you're reading, check out his reasons for saying you don't need more than "he said", "she said", if you need them at all. There really is little point in my quoting what he's already written about so well. It's all in his book.

Well, I have only one other cardinal rule when it comes to editing. If my first rule was

DON'T EDIT WHILE YOU'RE WRITING

My second rule is

EDIT YOUR WRITING BY READING IT ALOUD

I cannot emphasize strongly enough how much easier and quicker editing becomes, at least in the initial stages, when you read ALOUD what you have written. I have been doing it throughout writing this book. I may not do it the day I write a chapter or two, as I don't edit while writing. But the next time I return to the script, I read the previous work aloud.

This has become an invaluable part of my personal editing process. I both see and hear mistakes; I catch sentences that are just a bit too long to be completely coherent; I hear where I've repeated words more than once in longer paragraphs; my ears know when something isn't sitting properly or isn't saying what I want it to. Reading aloud to myself is the sharpest editing tool I have. My eyes never spot the flaws as quickly as my ears do.

How do other writers feel about reading what you've written aloud?

"Print it out; read it out loud and edit again". (Stephen King)

"Good writers of prose must be part poet, always listening to what they write." (William Zinsser)

"As the story moves forward, I read my work aloud to hear how it sounds. And for good reason. I can read my work silently and think it reads just fine, but when I hear it, I am often disappointed. In those early stages, the work is one giant ball of challenges: it's too wordy, it's lackluster, it's without emotion, there's too little dialog, too much dialog, the pacing is off, the sentences are awkward, and so forth" (Pam Munoz Ryan, Author of **Esperanza Rising**, **The Dreamer**)

Need more reasons for reading out loud?

When you read aloud and stumble over the words, you know immediately something isn't working. You can hear and/or pick up mistakes in grammar, punctuation and meaning. If you find yourself pausing in your oral reading, it could be a sign you need to insert a comma. Perhaps you even need to end the sentence. Periods keep separate thoughts from running into each other. You'll also become aware of what is known as "run-on" sentences. Those can be really annoying to a reader who knows grammar, and there are still a few of us around.

And heaven forbid, but if you're reading your story out loud to yourself and lose track of where it's going, or find yourself getting bored, that's a huge sign you've got some serious editing to do. It means you've been inserting filler and throw away lines. That's the stuff readers will start skipping over.

Those have to go! After all, if you find what you're reading boring, how will your reader feel?

When it comes to memoir, I believe reading out loud is doubly important for one simple reason: voice. Your voice. When you read out loud, you will know if what you hear is your voice or someone else's. Everything in your memoir should reflect your perspective, your personality. This is YOUR story, your memoir.

Reading out loud will let you know conclusively if there is ME in your MEmoir. The voice you hear should be YOURS. According to James Scott Bell, author of **"Voice: The Secret Power of Great Writing":**

"Voice is crucial. It takes you from skillful, competent, literate and forgettable to the kind of book we all love to find-unputdownable."

Before you decide your memoir is ready for publication (if that is your intention), answer these questions below:

Does your memoir tell the truth as closely as you remember it?

Does every page drive one single story forward?

Is every event interesting and necessary to your story? Will your story suffer if you take it out?

Have you used Dialogue, and Showing instead of telling, to reveal character?

If your family is involved in any way in the memoir you plan to publish, are you ready and able to cope with any flack that your memoir may generate?

If, and when you can put a checkmark beside each of the points above, you are ready to share your MEmoir at last.

I cannot leave this chapter without adding this:

If you choose to write your memoir freely with abandonment, as I've suggested throughout this book, I cannot, and will not guarantee you'll end up with a literary masterpiece, an award-winner or a best seller. All I am offering you is a way that works for many memoir writers, and given that writing memoir is giving readers a very personal close-up into your life, a "selfie" as it were, this genre almost begs to be told in a conversational style. So the more readers feel like this is YOU talking with them, (not educating or preaching to them), the more they will enjoy your book and identify with YOU, because you have put "ME" in your Memoir.

14 BACK TO YOUR FUTURE MEMOIR

At a guess, depending on how quickly you read this book...in one day? in several? in a month or more...your mind must be spinning a bit. It wouldn't surprise me either if by now, that inner critic you wrote to back in Chapter 5, is paying you a return visit.

So do yourself, and me, a favor right now: put down this book; pick up your pen and paper and jot down all your thoughts, both negative and positive. Include anything that inner critic is whispering in your ear.

Write it freely, organically, with abandon. I'm not there looking over your shoulder. You don't have to share it with me or anyone. Let it all out. And when you're done, read it...OUT LOUD. Decide if you like what you are telling yourself. What you hear yourself saying will determine if there really is a MEmoir in your future.

Done?

So, is there a MEmoir in your future?

What kind is it? Is it an autobiography made up of lots of little stories you want to leave as a legacy for your family?

If so, then by now you're probably hoping I'll give you that one thing folks love getting at those workshops: writing prompts.

Sorry. Not going to do that. And my reason is the same as that given by Marion Roach Smith (***www.marionroach.com***) who's been teaching memoir writing for years.

On her website, Marion bluntly states she feels all those writing prompts are a waste of time. Why? Because all her classes are *"filled with people recovering from those very exercises, people whose sole relationship to writing was practicing, not writing for real."*

That's exactly what I told you about in Chapter 4: those folks who kept coming back to my workshops but who, except for a couple, never ended up writing a book.

What did they come back for again and again? I'd love to say it's because they found me so entertaining, motivating, inspiring. However, I suspect it's more likely they returned for the repeated pleasure they felt in being part of a writing group; they enjoyed the mental stimulation, the social interaction.

There's nothing wrong with that at all, but, **"Don't write your MEmoir without ME"** was written for those with a specific reason for writing a memoir.

Those people, like Barbara Studham, author of **"Two Decades of Diapers"** and **"Fetal Alcohol Syndrome: The Teen Years"**, didn't return for the next session. They were busy writing their memoirs!

So, at this point, we reach a fork in the road toward the conclusion of this book. I offer you these two choices:

CHOICE #1:

If you don't have a specific story to tell, but you feel, after what you've read in this book, that you'd like to get more practice at writing with abandon, then all you need to do at this time is search Google for "memoir writing prompts". That search will drag up pages of links containing prompts. Or, you could go further, and buy a neat little book I've used in my classes titled **"Lifetales Workbook"** by Karen Hamilton Silvestri. It's chock-a-block with prompts and what Karen calls "memory sparklers".

Go for broke! Write as many stories as you can. Write them organically, freely, with abandon. No editing as you go, okay? Enjoy how the process opens up memories when you're free of the constraints that have held you back in the past: your inner critic and all those rules you learned at school about how to write properly. Enjoy the sensation as the words, your thoughts and feelings land, unbridled, uncensored on the page.

And if it so happens that what you end up with is a great collection of stories you decide to publish as a book, please let me know. I'd love to hear from you.

You can contact me via my personal author's website at *http://www.vigaboland.com*, or my writer support sites, *Memoirabilia* and *Vianvi.*

CHOICE #2:

The second choice is for those of you who picked up this book because you already had a story you knew you had to tell or wanted to share. You had a **purpose** for writing a memoir. You just needed a nudge, some help in getting started and past those obstacles that have been holding you back.

I truly hope everything I've shared till now has shown you a way to do that. It worked for me and I know it works for others, whether they are famous writers like Stephen King, or still to become famous writers like my fellow authors, Barbara Studham, Toni Pacini and Daliah Husu, just to name a few.

In preparation for this book, I asked several of these authors to share their writing process. The first of these ladies is Barbara Studham who has now written three memoirs and over half a dozen fiction books since she attended my first workshop in 2014. In a "homework" assignment I gave the group in that first workshop, Barbara wrote her story, **"Sooty"**. When she finished reading to the group, you could have heard a pin drop. You can read "Sooty" in the section of this book, *"Memoirabilia Advice and Feature Stories",* reprints from my Memoirabilia magazine.

Below is what Barbara shared about writing "Sooty" and how she writes all her books today:

> *"How did I write it? I remember that Sooty incident coming to me when you asked us to write information in our decades bank. That was one that stood out during my first ten years of age bank. Yes, I just let it flow because I wanted to get it out of my system and onto paper. I don't think I edited it until after I realized it had an impact on the group. To me it was just part of my life, not really worth sharing, but that changed when I saw the look on the group's faces when I read it aloud. At first, I thought they went silent because they thought it was boring, but*

after hearing the gasps of shock, I realized I had a story to write.

Although I had already written fiction before attending your memoir sessions, writing memoir is far different than writing fiction, as it has to be truthful, interesting, and have a strong subject matter with dialogue. To help compile my memoir, I wrote all the vignettes first, edited them, then wrote my story around them.

Another important aspect was doing the assignments you gave us. My vignettes evolved from there.

With my fiction books, I just write and the story reveals itself. I consider the story the skeleton. When I have the skeleton, I go back to the beginning and add muscle, appearance, etc. It depends on how long I leave it before editing. Sometimes I begin a new book and get involved with that story before returning to the first one and editing. It is best to leave it alone for a while as the errors glare when you read it through new eyes. Also, I like to read it aloud to myself, especially where the dialogue is concerned as I want it to sound as real as possible."

As you can see, the prolific Barbara Studham does several things I'm recommending in this book: she writes freely with abandon and edits later; she leaves her work to ferment for a while before editing; and she reads what she's written out loud.

Toni Pacini, author of the memoir, **"Alabama Blue"** also heads up writers' groups in Las Vegas. Toni must be a riot in her workshops if she's anything like the voice we can hear below as she shares how she wrote "Alabama Blue". Enjoy!

"First of all, the writing of Alabama Blue was VERY different from how I write today. I have wanted to write AB, seriously wanted to write it and not just jibber-jabber about it, for 30-years. I started it then, writing little snippets of memory. Sometimes on cocktail napkins. Always pen to paper. Unfortunately I frequently destroyed my work due to my own lack of self worth and shame. But I slowly realized that although it was hard to

write about, I felt better when I did.

I am and always have written by the seat of my britches, yep, a pantster. Sometimes I am more anal than others and stop every couple of pages to re-read, re-write. Sometimes I just let it go and pour out like that delicious vanilla soft-serve ice cream Mickey D's sells. I love it when it flows full and fast and almost starts piling up on top of itself in a swirl of words, like a well turned cone. Crap...now I'm hungry!

AB was written in pieces and parts from 1986 until April 8, 2016 ~ The day before it was published. I actually did physical cut and paste (or tape) for years. I would decide that the 16th page should go to page 42, etc., I had a mess. HA In 1996 I really pulled it together and had over 100 hand written taped together pages and a woman I cared for, Rose, I did non-medical hospice care at the time, told her family to give me her Web TV system when she died.

They did and I was thrilled. Today that little thing seems so silly, but I taught myself to type on it and learned about Cyber-Space. A year later I bought a used computer and typed in all the work I had done. In typed form it was only about 50 pages, which really pissed me off.

I got serious in 1997-1998 and kicked butt. I had written and rewritten just over 100 pages when the computer froze up, pooped out, Yikes. I lost it all and I had destroyed my written pages once they were in the computer. I was new to computers and did not understand how to save my work to (it was disk then) so I was devastated and vowed to never write another page.

It's obviously too late to make a long story short, but since I just published AB, clearly I got back to it. I learned and never lost my work again. So from 1999 until I met Walt in 2004, I wrote and re-wrote AB, I never thought it was good enough to share. But I kept at it."

Toni's story shows you what a difference having a purpose, a reason for writing a memoir means. When you have a reason to write, and you know that both you and others will benefit from reading your memoir, you write it come hell or high water and regardless how long it takes. Toni's perseverance paid off. "Alabama Blue" is a poignant, touching memoir with lots of "ME" in it, just like Barbara Studham's books on FASD. And as she told us, she, like me, just writes, letting it *"pour out like delicious vanilla soft serve"*. What a great analogy Toni.

Daliah Husu has just published her first memoir, **"I am Woman"**. You will find my review of her very revealing and honest memoir about transitioning from male to female in the book review section of my **Vianvi** website. Just like Barbara's and Toni's, Daliah's memoir was one I couldn't put down, not just because of the riveting subject matter, but because of how much ME was in her memoir. She didn't hold back on what must have been a very painful story to share with the world. That's the way to do it, to get "ME" into your MEmoir. Remember what C.S. Larkin said in her book, **"Shoot Your Novel"**:

"Readers want to be immersed in story and character, and you can't achieve that by holding them at arm's length—or relegating them to standing a hundred yards away."

So how did Daliah do it?

> *"I wrote most of my material as it came to my head, but my thought process followed chronologically with my life story so I did not have to do much thinking of what came next. Occasionally, I would move paragraphs around for better flow. I do stop to reread what I just wrote and make minimal changes but I find that I get sidetracked if I try to edit too early on in the process. I only stop to think if I have not already drafted that particular chapter's story line."*

A final comment on how well freely writing with abandonment works comes from Dr. Gulara Vincent, who is a huge fan of Barbara Turner Vesselago, author of **"Writing Without a**

Parachute". Gulara was mentored by Barbara for a year after attending one of her workshops. Very recently, Gulara wrote a blog post on overcoming writer's block. Here's how she gets past that block and starts writing again when it happens:

> *"Last year, I was working with a writing mentor. Every month, I had to write up two 12-page submissions. Some pieces were not difficult to write. I had an idea, and writing it up was just a matter of finding time and space. Other times, I resisted with all my might, because either what I was about to write was too painful, or because I put pressure on myself to produce the next piece before the deadline."*

To get out of the writer's block, here's what Gulara did:

> *"I sat at my computer and started writing up the sensations I felt in my body. The more I dropped into my body, the better was the flow until I found myself writing up a memory I would have dismissed because it didn't feel significant enough. The result was always surprising. In fact, this is how I've written some of my favorite pieces."* *(https://gularavincent.com)*

Well, there you have it. I truly believe, and these three writers are proof, that when it comes to memoirs, writing freely, organically with abandonment works. It worked for them. It worked for me. It will work for you if you let it.

If you really want to write your memoir, have a story to tell, and a reason for writing it, embrace the challenge I'm giving you here today:

Put "ME" into your MEmoir and write a memoir others want to read

15 NAILING THE "ME" IN YOUR MEMOIR

It should be becoming clear to you by now, after reading what other writers have shared above, that if you truly want to write a memoir and can state a reason, a purpose for doing so, by writing organically, freely, with abandon in the initial stages you will get your memoir written. Period. And as long as you don't edit yourself out of your memoir during the editing stage, you will have put ME into your MEmoir.

That said, it's now time to zero in on YOUR memoir. Begin by recording your responses to the questions below. Take your time with this. Think through each response carefully, and above all, honestly. There is no point lying to yourself. You do not have to explain your answers, or show them to anyone. So for that matter, don't write your answers in the margins of this book!

Answering the questions below will help you separate what, and who, are important to keeping your story moving forward. These will make you a bit more aware of the little "asides", those "babies" Stephen King warned about, that are special to you, but not the reader.

Are you ready? Let's go!

1) What is your purpose (i.e. motive, reason) for writing your memoir?
2) Apart from yourself, who do you hope will read it?
3) What's the benefit to YOU of writing your memoir?
4) How do you feel your memoir will benefit others?
5) What story (plot, situation) is key to your memoir?
6) Who, apart from yourself, is an essential part of the story?
7) Who are the lesser players in your memoir?
8) Who is responsible for the situation on which your memoir is based?
9) What factors contributed to this situation?
10) What are the key struggles faced by you or others in your memoir?
11) How did you cope with the struggles, and who, if anyone helped you resolve them? How?

12) In every story, fiction or memoir, there are crises, highpoints. List some of these crises in your story.

13) Think about "turning points" in your life. List those.

14) Now, what is the one crucial incident, the one event that turned everything around, that led you to make life changing, albeit painful decisions?

15) Once those decisions were made, and you acted upon them, how did you feel?

Lastly, have a go at this popular exercise given by memoir writing coaches everywhere: **tell your life story in exactly six words**!

Impossible you say? Legend has it Ernest Hemingway did it with this 6-word sentence: *"For Sale: baby shoes; never worn."*

There's actually a website devoted to these 6-word memoirs: **http://www.sixwordmemoirs.com**

Check it out. Fascinating. Here's a few more examples from a magazine, **"It all changed in an instant"** published by the folks behind that site:

"Found on Craigslist: table, apartment, fiance" © Becki Lee

"After cancer, I became a semicolon." © Anthony R. Cardno

Aren't they clever? They'd make great book titles too.

I cannot finish up this book without addressing one of the most difficult parts of writing memoir: **facing painful memories**. The inability or reluctance to face painful memories is a principal reason some people decide not to write their memoirs after attending a ton of workshops and reading lots of how-to books. I've had workshop participants burst into tears when I asked them to write freely (and privately) about the *"most painful experience they've ever had",* or about *"the one thing you could never share with anyone."* These are loaded prompts. Writers have told me they wrote their memoirs with tears pouring onto the page along with the words. They've had to stop, walk away from the writing, and pull themselves together before continuing. At times like that, the inner critic roars in their heads screaming at them to stop this madness called memoir writing. Some do stop and shelve the book forever.

I have no magic solution for how you can get past breaking down while writing. Perhaps, if it's that hard, you are not yet ready to write and share your pain. But I came across something three years ago written by Adair Lara, author of **"Make your Memoir Suck Less"** and **"Naked, Drunk and Driving"** that really hit home:

"When you pin your misfortune to a page, you rob it of its power. You begin to get distance from an event the moment you write it down. Even the most intimate and horrendous details of your life become transformed into material."

Adair also shared this:

"You could be contemplating suicide as did Tim O'Brien, author of "The Things they Carried". As he thought about it, he wrote about it. "I'd literally leave the typewriter and go to the balcony, and think about jumping off, and go back and type another sentence!"

Wow...just wow! I have repeated those sentences to every group in every workshop since.

If you are ready to "pin your misfortune to a page" and rob it of its power over you, you will write that "ME" into your MEmoir.

The result? A timeless **"Selfie in Words"** created by YOU.

16. YOUR MEMOIR: "A SELFIE IN WORDS"

Your Memoir

A selfie in words

©Viga Boland, 2015

www.memoirabilia.ca

At the beginning of **"Don't Write Your Memoir without ME!"** and here and there throughout the book, I indicated my belief that your memoir is a **"selfie in words"**. As much as I dislike that popular social media practice of posting "selfies", the term is incredibly appropriate to understanding what you are doing when you put truly put "ME" into your Memoir.

Just like those selfies on Facebook or Instagram, when you write a **ME**moir you are exposing yourself to the world. You are risking criticism, but for more than just your looks or assumed vanity in putting yourself "out there" nearly naked.

Once you choose to bare your heart, mind and soul in words, you need to be ready for what the world will throw at you, both good and bad. When I wrote **"No Tears for my Father"**, my own true story of incest, I was scared, not of what my family might think as my parents had both passed away years before, and my living husband and children had encouraged me to tell my story, but of how readers would perceive my role in that story.

As it turned out, I had a right to be worried. I copped comments from men like

"How nice of you to speak this way about your father. He's not here to defend himself. How do we know you didn't want or ask for what he gave you?"

Do you know how much comments like that hurt? Or how about this one left by a woman in an Amazon review of my book:

"I am ashamed that this woman never held her father accountable for his actions. Her weakness in her situation is unbelievable."

Others, younger readers, questioned why I had kept my silence for nearly 45 years. They couldn't understand why I hadn't gone to my school guidance counselors, or as an adult, to women's shelters or ultimately to the police. Of course. How could they understand my "weakness", my failure to act? My story took place in the late 50's to 60's when there were no such services available to victims of abuse.

Still others blasted my mother for her failure to help me. They assumed, naturally, and wrongly, that she knew the incest was occurring and did nothing about it. I had told my story with complete honesty, yet found myself needing to vindicate not only myself but my mother, who was herself a pathetic and broken victim of my father's physical and mental abuse.

And the biggest reason for these negative responses was one of the primary reasons why I had to write that "selfie in words": to enlighten the unenlightened about those situations we humans would rather not discuss, or choose to hide or deny... those situations that destroy the lives of children worldwide daily: child sexual abuse. It's ugly; it's real; and someone must speak for those who cannot speak for themselves.

I chose to be one of those people, to become a voice for the voiceless, by writing my **ME**moir. Was it easy? No. But was it rewarding? In more ways than I could ever say, especially when the positive feedback so outweighed the few negative responses. It reminds me of that adage:

"No monuments were ever erected to critics, only to those who were criticized'

As much as I love having the last word, I'd like to leave you with the following words of wisdom from my friend, **Denis Ledoux of The Memoir Network**. What he shares below supports much of the argument I've presented in this book for putting **ME** into your **ME**moir by writing freely, organically and with abandonment when you first begin writing that memoir. The result will be a more personal memoir of greater universal meaning and relevance. It may not win an award, but it will win hearts.

******

Seven Reasons for Writing a More Personal Memoir

You must not resist writing a more personal memoir.

You want to write your memoir, but you resist getting too personal, going in too deep.

Your guarded secret that you wanted to have your own business one day or your hope that your father would apologize eventually for his denigration of you—this has happened and it has had a great impact on you. Your even deeper secrets—the sexual orientation that you dared not reveal or your negative self-concept—surely this can't be the subject of a memoir. How would you live this down? Isn't it better to stick with the facts and dates? And aren't these inner realities too personal to impose on others?

1) The more personal your memoir the more universal it is.

The personal, honestly described, is often the most universal. If there is a place where it is important to acknowledge, "This is who I really was and who I really am," where you need share with others the hero's journey you have undertaken —successful or not, it is in your memoir. Here, the inner changes, the emotional turmoil, the psychological victories, defeats and challenges that have made you the person you are today will speak to your readers. Without this sort of personal material, your memoir will be less universal, less interesting—for you to write and for others to read.

2) The more personal memoir, the one that records inner experience, creates peace for the writer.

While writing your story, you will gain understanding and appreciation for the journey you have taken; you will appreciate the uniqueness of your responses to people, events and developments. So many people have said to me, "Writing my story has helped me to accept what was." Others have commented on how it is like therapy. And being at peace you will not need to hide the experience that will make your story appealing.

3) Your story well told stimulates personal growth.

If you have not always lived your life wisely, what better time than now to come to terms with that? Lifewriting offers you the chance to examine patterns of behavior and attitudes that shaped your past and to explore how to alter these as you go about being yourself in the present. Fresh insights gained from lifewriting will infuse your awareness. Your writing—the act itself and the resulting stories—will allow you to see and utilize new ways of being that serve not just survival but becoming fully yourself. It's time to stop living other people's dreams and to explore yours. This desire for fulfillment is a universal one, and your reader will find self-recognition in reading your experience.

4) Your story will mentor your readership.

I believe one of the reasons readers pick up a memoir is in order to be mentored. Your readers will be guided by your personal tale as you point out pitfalls and opportunities from your life experience. By not holding back in revealing the whole of your *story—the inner as well as the outer story, you reassure and guide readers as they make their own ways through life. By being brave enough to write your inner truth, you mentor your audience. The dates and facts alone aren't enough to do that.*

5) **Your courageous example will embolden future generations.**

Your written inner story portrays the particulars of being the person you are and it will survive you. Your understanding of your inner life will help your descendants and future readers to appreciate their own existence. Don't shortchange yourself and your family with a memoir that is just a chronology of dates and facts. There is so much more that posterity deserves, and needs, to know!

6) **Even if your secrets remain secrets from us, writing them will work its magic on you.**

Remember: it's okay to write about your pain and your anguish, your foolishness and inadequacies, and to decide not to publish this story of your inner life for anyone to read! You don't have to share what you write unless you want to. Once you have benefited from the insights you've gained, you can destroy any piece of writing you wish to destroy or store it where only you will see it. You are the first audience for your book—and that's a very important audience. So even if you do not publish your story for others, you have written it for a very important reader—you. But, that said, you may want to think again about keeping your story too private.

Insights whether you publish them or not, are influencers of theme and are part of your story—even if only behind the scene. Because you have had an insight you will write differently from then on. The inner life, and its articulation, is always an influencer.

7) **Your insights, even not shared are essential to discovering your theme.**

The journey of exploration which is the memoir must necessarily go into the inner self. This journey is as old as the human race.

Writing your story is not vulgar or self-important and it is admittedly not easy. Rather, it is a commitment you make to your true self and a gift of understanding, guidance and reassurance you give to those who come after you.

You can succeed at writing an interesting and successful memoir. Just follow a few guidelines to help you succeed and don't forget to include your inner life.

© *Denis Ledoux, author, teacher,* **The Memoir Network**

http://thememoirnetwork.com/seven-reasons-write-personal-memoir/

****

Thanks for reading **"Don't Write Your MEmoir without ME!"** If you enjoyed it and think others might too, please leave me a review on my Author's website at ***www.vigaboland.com*** my other sites at **Memoirabilia** and **Vianvi**, along with other online distribution sites where you may have purchased this book.

In the following sections of this book, you will find additional MEMOIR WRITING ADVICE, featured STORIES, book EXCERPTS and REVIEWS originally published in my printed and online magazine, MEMOIRABILIA.

At the end of the book is a READING and SITE-SEEING RESOURCE section and a little more ABOUT THE AUTHOR of this book, me, Viga Boland.

FURTHER ADVICE & THOUGHTS

From contributors to

MEMOIRABILIA

http://www.memoirabilia.ca

FREEFALL WRITING
By Barbara Turner Vesselago

Freefall Writing™, the approach to writing that I have evolved over the past three decades, does not concern itself with style, punctuation, or even the conventions of genre. Those are the old chestnuts, easy enough to learn when the time seems appropriate. My purpose is to help writers trust the writing process and interact with it as they write, rather than trying to control it. The resulting ring of authority, unique to every writer, translates to the reader as "voice." To the writer, it feels more like absorption – a deep and vibrant connection with whatever is being written.

Writers can take this newfound trust in writing in whatever direction their aspirations lie. As one writer reported after a recent workshop in Newmarket:

I experienced a dramatic shift in perspective. I knew I had been missing something in the novel I had just written, and now I had it. It was that quality of being truly "in" a character; of inhabiting them. So that their life is your life, and all past, present and future can be drawn upon at any given moment to inform and enrich the story, to create shadows and point a finger. I thought I was well in, but this workshop with you allowed me to see what I had been missing.

How does this deepening take place? First of all, I believe that in order to do enough writing for it to become truly powerful (and therefore publishable), writers have to become engrossed in it. I also know from experience that much of what happens in writing comes from somewhere beyond the conscious mind. To get out of my own way and let that happen, I almost have to trick myself. Absorption is the key.

Five basic precepts will help any writer to be swept away. First, sit down without a plan, and write what comes up for you. Second, don't change anything. Just leave what you're writing on the page. Be sure to give all the sensuous details (#3) (the words of W.O. Mitchell, to whom I am indebted for an early version of this process). This will immediately pull you in further. Go where the energy is (#4) for you as you write, or if that's not clear, "go fearward." Write what you don't want to write. And if "what comes up" is autobiographical, know that if it's 10 years old, it works better (#5). It will have "composted," as Natalie Goldberg says, becoming fertile and ready to use.

Here is a brief example of where these precepts first took one writer:

I am making our bed, in our shared bedroom, an old Victorian home, 18 inch thick walls, bluestone foundations, high red carpeted stairs, little piles of clothes always on the lower steps ready to be taken upstairs by anybody planning the ascent. Those stairs seemed so high sometimes and five of us slept upstairs so there were many things in transit.

I smooth the bottom sheet and plump the big pillows, begin to shake the down blanket. Tears are starting to trickle from my eyes onto the bed, our shared abode of companionship, of love. Aubrey, a neighbor and doctor, had called by that morning. He said my tests did not really show anything, not arthritis, not tendonitis in my wrists, so what was wrong? Why am I so tired? Why are my torn hands so sore, my feet so tender and sensitive, inflamed, red, so stiff? He looked deeply into my face: "A friend of mine has Scleroderma," he said. "I think that is what it might be."

I tell Bruce, now on the opposite side of the bed, pulling up the other side of the quilt. "How long have we got?" he asks softly. "I don't know," comes out automatically. "It depends on whether the skin within my kidneys and lungs becomes affected, Aubrey says."

He approaches me as if with fear and love: "Are you still there", in his arms as they enfold my weak body. "We'll do anything you want together, travel together, we'll take the children." He is frightened. I cannot see beyond today.

In this moving piece, I can feel the writer approach and back away, recycling a few thoughts ("those thick walls – symbolic?"), perhaps digressing a little. Moving fearward, she returns to the scene that's unfolding. Again the urge to explain surfaces ("our shared abode," etc.), but she shrugs it off and enters the current: the news, and the couple taking it in, forced by this great unknown to enter the present moment.

Writing like this makes me think of holding your hand in the fire: you stay with it only as long as you can bear. But the next time, you can do it longer. When this subject comes up again for this writer, there's no sign of backing away:

I am breathing heavily, conscious I must keep breathing, gasping, panic, my life, breathe, my body is becoming cold, colder, cold through to my bones, painful cold, white surrounds me, it is snow I think, I am lying in it, cold pain, my horse hurt nearby. I cannot help the others now. Will I be caught? Will I die? Breathe. Cold, cold to my bones.

"Help, help me, I am still alive."

Somebody is beside me, his hand is burning on my heart, it feels like a hot coal on my body.

"Where are you, Margaret? Speak to me from where you are."

"I am in the snow, lying, I thought I was going to die, there was nobody to help. If I had called they would have caught me so I would have died anyway – "

"And you did call."

"Yes, and here you are, and I am alive."

So many times I have been sick with the fear of cold, crying with the pain in my body, in my hands, my feet, holding my breath in shock as my hands go blue and then white, drawing the blood from my skin in terror, my husband holding me in love and care, not knowing, not understanding.

That pain and those fears of cold have slipped by me now.

My terror doesn't draw the blood from my hands. Now my skin is much stronger and softer and pink, and mostly warm. I can sit on the point in the soft wind and know that my husband is across the sea, waiting for my return. I hear the birds tentatively accept my being here, then relax as they prepare and call.

By now she is able, unflinchingly, to inhabit this former self. The awkward syntax is gone, the voice clear, and that lovely last line reflects true spontaneity: I'm sure it was nowhere in her mind when she started.

As she keeps writing, these strengths will become ingrained, and easy to invoke on behalf of another character. And she will keep writing. As the writer from Newmarket went on to say, that's another great gift of this process: "It continues to pour out, so many words jostling to be next on the line... a river of words tumbling over rocks and fallen trees. Yippee, they say, I'm free!"

© Barbara Turner Vesselago,
http://www.freefallwriting.com

(This article was originally published by Viga Boland in Memoirabilia Magazine, Issue #5, October 2015)

FIVE WAYS TO WRITE A MEMOIR WITHOUT BEING DISOWNED
By Linda Robinson Brendle

Anaiah Press published my memoir, *A Long and Winding Road: A Caregiver's Tale of Life, Love, and Chaos,* on July 1, 2014. As the release day drew near, they posted the first chapter on their blog. I received some nice feedback and also some questions. Here are two of the more interesting ones:

How did you find the courage to write a memoir?...My family would have me excommunicated!

Did you share details with your family while you were writing the book?

I fired off a short version of an Anne Lamott quote: *"If they didn't want me to write about them, they should have behaved better."* Still, the questions lingered in my mind, so I developed a list of ways to write a memoir and still maintain family harmony.

Know your motives

Why are you writing your story? Do you have a specific goal, or do you just want to air your dirty laundry? There is a market for both types of memoir, but the first is less likely to lead to trouble.

When I first became a caregiver, my aunt suggested I keep a journal. Initially, it was a place to vent when things became tense, but then I gathered my courage and shared some of my writing. People sometimes laughed or cried with me, and some said, *"Thanks, I thought I was the only one."* By the time I began working on my memoir, I had a purpose - to amuse, encourage, and maybe even inspire both caregivers and others going caught in difficult circumstances. Hopefully, I haven't stepped on too many toes in the process.

Tell your own story

Studies in conflict resolution often focus on "I" messages. In any disagreement, it is important to speak about your own actions and feelings instead of assigning blame to others. I feel hurt when no one notices the clean house is much better than You always make a mess, and you never notice when I clean it up. In writing my memoir, I tried to tell my own story and leave others to tell theirs.

When I did cross over into a really personal story about someone else - like my son's struggle with depression or my brother's major clash with Dad - I asked for their approval. The exceptions were Mom and Dad. They were very private people and would probably have been embarrassed by having people read about them. However, by the time I realized people might actually be reading what I had written, they were too far into their dementia to understand, so I didn't ask. After lots of prayer and consultation with people who loved all of us, I decided that the result of helping others justified telling their story along with mine. I hope they agree or at least will have forgiven me by the time I see them again.

Make your characters likeable

After I began working with Jessica Schmeidler, my awesome editor at Anaiah, the reality of being published set in. I worried about the legal and ethical side of writing about real people, even if I was only including them as a part of my own story. I wondered if I should contact each person I mentioned, use pseudonyms, or just take my chances. Jessica wasn't concerned. *"I like all your characters,"* she said, *"so I don't see why anyone would be offended."* In writing a memoir, a writer is not creating characters. However, she does have the ability to make her characters sympathetic or not, depending on how she presents them.

Forgive before you write

In the Sermon on the Mount, Jesus said a person should not offer a gift at the altar until conflicts with others have been resolved. When you sit down to write about a person who has hurt you, it is important to forgive that person before you put your hands on the keyboard. As the author, you have complete control and can tell your story so that your readers will understand without a doubt who the injured party was and who the villain was. Regardless of which path you choose, you also must be prepared to accept the consequences. If you choose to exact vengeance, you must decide if vindication is worth becoming the pariah of the family.

Speak the truth in love

Finally, tell the truth as lovingly as you can. At some point in my caregiving journey, Mom and Dad became The Kids. It was a loving term that I used with friends and family, but once again I was worried about the reaction of a wider audience. I consulted my husband, my pastor, my editor, and even my blog readers about whether the nickname might be offensive. Generally, those who didn't know me personally said it was disrespectful, but those who knew how much I loved my parents saw no disrespect. Eventually, Jessica and I tweaked my story to make my intent clear, but she was not worried. *"Linda, your love and care for your parents is so obvious that I don't think anyone will misunderstand."*

If the author of a memoir skirts the truth in order to spare feelings, her story will not ring true. On the other hand, as she tells the truth, she must do so with love.

©Linda Robinson Brendle,
www.lifeaftercaregiving.wordpress.com

(This article was originally published by Viga Boland in Memoirabilia Magazine, Issue #5, October 2015)

REWORK YOUR STORY to
GET MORE SHOW and LESS TELL
By Denis Ledoux of The Memoir Network

There are ways to rework your stories so that you can minimize "telling" and maximize "showing." The biggest "telling" offense is perhaps the overuse of descriptive adjectives and adverbs.

Adjectives and adverbs often tell the reader what to feel or how to interpret the story instead of evoking that feeling and interpretation. While adjectives may seem to add color and movement and insight to a scene or description, they are often simply a lazy way to write. This is especially true of descriptive adjectives adjectives like beautiful and kind and nice!

One possible solution to this problem is not especially difficult. Replace at least half of your descriptive adjectives and adverbs with settings, dialogue, and actions.

Yes, half. That's 50%.

Here are examples of how to convert adjectives and adverbs into more effective writing:
Into ACTION:

She said angrily might become: *she said, picking up the mail and tearing it into shreds.*

Into SETTING:

We were poor might become: In the living room, the linoleum rug was ripped along the edges and black streak marks showed where the boards beneath were uneven.

Into DIALOGUE:

She was passive-aggressive might become: *She said, "I'm not angry. I haven't given it a second thought, you bastard"*

Whenever I present this option in a workshop, someone says, *"But you tell us all the time to be more concise in our writing. In fact, you have the 10% rule that we need to eliminate that much from our text before we turn it out on the world. What gives?"*

They're just different rules. The reworking I'm suggesting here does not produce a shorter more economical text. In fact, it usually results in a longer text. Length is not its goal. More evocative writing is. Replacing 50% of your descriptive adjectives with dialog and action produces a more impactful text.

Try it and see if you don't like the results.

©Denis Ledoux, *The Memoir Network*
http://thememoirnetwork.com

(This article was originally published by Viga Boland in Memoirabilia Magazine, Issue #5, October 2015)

HOW SHOULD YOU WRITE YOUR
MEMOIR? LIKE AN EDITOR WOULD!
by Rachelle Gardner

So you've written the last words of your memoir, put it away for 6 weeks, taken it back out, chopped out paragraphs, scenes, done spell & grammar checks, and now you're ready to send it to a publisher, or literary agent or self-publish. Wait! Are you sure it's ready for publication? Below, according to Rachelle Gardner, an agent with Books and Such Literary Agency, is what a good editor will do to your manuscript.

A good editor would have coached the author to find his main theme, and to focus tightly on it, cutting out rabbit trails and eliminating entertaining stories that didn't fit in this book. The editor could have helped decide which stories should stay and which should go (often difficult for a memoirist, because they're so close to the material).

An editor would have conveyed that teaching and preaching don't belong in a memoir. Save that for another book — a how-to or self-help. The memoir is your story and your reflections on your story, but should avoid the self-help vibe.

An editor would have eliminated bragging, and suggested ways to convey moments of success or triumph without sounding arrogant.

An editor would have brought out the importance of a humble tone, of admitting the journey isn't over and you're still learning, a sort of "fellow pilgrim" approach. When your story is nothing but triumph and "look what a great thing I did," real people don't tend to relate to your message.

An editor would have challenged the author to truly let the reader in. Authenticity and vulnerability are hallmarks of powerful memoirs, and this one has neither. I had the feeling of skimming over the surface, never quite being allowed in.

An editor would have ensured readers didn't feel like complete losers if they don't currently share the author's lifestyle.

An editor would have protected the author's reputation. The author conveyed a message he may not have intended by including certain observations and behaviors unrelated to the theme of the book, but which made him seem like a womanizer and a bit of a sexist. A savvy editor would have gently inquired if this was really what the author wanted readers to take away.

So now, after reading Rachelle's comments, is your memoir really ready for the scrutiny of a publisher or literary agent? Is it really what those who don't know you will be interested in, and want to read? This is the time to get really tough with yourself. Chop out the unnecessary. Cut the padding. Stop with the teaching, preaching and coaching. Remember, a MEMOIR IS A STORY first and foremost! Thanks Rachelle Gardner for the reminder.

Learn more from Rachelle at
http://www.rachellegardner.com

This article was originally published, with permission, by Viga Boland in Memoirabilia Magazine, Issue #3, May 2015

IT'S ABOUT CHANNELING YOUR CONFLICT

By Tana Bevan

http://www.tanasworld.com

Speak to me, oh Muse of writing,
For certain you are there,
(though occupied with others),
perhaps you've time to spare?

If you find yourself wanting to limit conflict at all costs — in your life or writing — you'll wind up limiting your potential, your life, and end up in Mediocrity. Since most conflicts in your life are with yourself, even if you don't want to deal with conflict, you're going to have to. Might as well get to it.

An alternative to the mediocrity and self-destructive behavior of your efforts and exertion to avoid conflicts and Self (drugs, alcohol, sugar, self-medicating, extreme behaviors, addictions, etc.), is taking pen in hand (crayon, pencil, or sitting in front of the keyboard also work) and letting it all out. Spew forth! Let all the bilge and bile rush out. Keep at it until the initial onslaught slows to a trickle. Once you're in trickle-mode and have a routine going, find some nuggets of gold in the free-flowing bilge. Those nuggets will be worth exploring. Spending time with. Getting to know.

Disclaimer: The process of growing is obnoxious. It hurts. It's painful. It's a drag. Still, the results are sooooo worth it. You acquire an expanded world view. Energy surges. You gain purpose. A sense of well being. A greater sense of Self. The best analogy I can offer is pregnancy. A horrible experience in my opinion. Giving birth is a really lousy end to nine lousy months. (Can you tell I had extremely difficult pregnancies?) But the end result is totally worth it. Even after the hell I went through, I wanted to do it again. And again. That's what growth is like. Sometimes that's what it takes to get the writing out. But once it's out. Once you've given it life. A whole chapter of Self opens before you.

Do your part by getting the bilge down to a dull roar. Pan for those nuggets of gold. Keep your ears (physical and other) tuned to the frequencies and make sure you transcribe what you hear.

Remember also, wherever you are in the process, keep an open invitation extended to your Muse.

Originally written for and published, with permission, by Viga Boland at http://www.vigaboland.com

WHAT DO WRITERS MOST NEED?
A DEEPLY, PERSONAL EMOTIONAL ANCHOR
by Viga Boland, author & editor *"Memoirabila"*

So what do writers most need? Is it all those books you keep buying about how to write or all those courses you keep taking? How many books about writing do you own? I must have 20 or more. But I think I can throw most of them away after reading what I did this morning. All I or you or most writers need is a "deeply, personal, emotional anchor". Let me explain.

What I'm about to share now isn't just for memoir writers. It's for writers of all genres. And I have to confess that what I want to tell you isn't original. I stole it. Or rather, what I read in this post by JAMES ALTUCHER, inspired me to write this post. Such good advice. Such insight. So damn right!

Maybe what I read in Altucher's post screamed so loudly at me because it justified my own style and approach to writing. I wrote all three of my memoirs without thinking of being the next Margaret Atwood or Ernest Hemingway. I didn't give much thought to using all the devices that the 20 or so books I own said I must. I just wrote. From the heart. With passion. I didn't care if my books became bestsellers or not. I didn't care if they won awards. I wrote them because I had a "deeply personal, emotional anchor" to what I was writing as a victim of childhood sexual abuse.

And here's the strange part: once my 3 memoirs were written and published, I swore those were the last memoirs I would write. I was done. So I waffled around trying to find something else to write about. My mind was blank. In desperation, I grabbed the pen and started writing a fiction piece. It took me twice as long to write that 7000 word short story as it took me to write "The Ladies of Loretto". But as I wrote, I realized something was happening to the characters in my fiction piece: they were extensions of the characters, the real people in my memoirs, especially of myself. What was this? Why was it so hard to keep sexual deviation out of my writing?

The answer came to me this morning in James Altucher's post. I am deeply, personally, emotionally anchored it that subject. And if it works for Kurt Vonnegut, JK Rowling, Stephen King to be deeply emotionally and personally anchored, why am I fighting it?

It it ain't broke, don't fix it, right?

So just what did Mr. Altucher say that so inspired and encouraged me about my writing today? Read his entire post at the link above, but here's the part that got me:

Here's what I think all great artists do:

They have a deeply personal emotional anchor they can tie their work to.

For Kurt Vonnegut, he was dramatically effected by the firebombing of Dresden, Germany, where he was a prisoner of war.

130,000 people died in a single day. Compared with 90,000 in Hiroshima. Kurt Vonnegut survived and his job after that was to dig up all the bodies.

When he ANCHORS a book (in Slaughterhouse Five, for instance, he anchors to the most horrific moment of his life – Dresden), he can go CRAZY after that: time travel, other planets, placing the author as a side character in the book, all sorts of experimentation.

It doesn't matter because he can always pull back to the emotional anchor when he needs to. And then we all relate.

No emotional anchor = no art. No meaning.

Another example: Harry Potter. The emotional anchor: an orphan, mistreated by step-parents, wants to feel special.

The craziness: Off to wizard's school to fight bad magic everywhere!

Another example: Carrie. Social outcast girl with overly religious and strict mother. Craziness: Rains blood on everyone at the prom.

None of these writers use fancy language. They get their emotional anchor. Then they go crazy. They are not "trained" writers. They write.

Oh I love what he said there! Read that last line again: *"None of these writers use fancy language. They get their emotional anchor. Then they go crazy. They are not "trained" writers. They write."*

YES, YES, and YES! I don't use fancy language. I do have an emotional anchor. I go a little crazy. I'm not a trained writer. I just write.

Get it? What's your deeply personal emotional anchor? That's the secret to writing that memoir or anything you're struggling to write. That's what writers most need.

Don't fight it. Don't edit it. Give in to it. Just let it flow. Just write!

©Viga Boland, *Memoirabilia Online Magazine*. August 3, 2015

http://www.memoirabilia.ca

http://www.vigaboland.com

http://www.vianvi.com

GREAT BEGINNINGS to MEMOIRS

Ever since I began running memoir writing workshops, I've been a follower of the newsletters, prompts and advice offered by **Matilda Butler & Kendra Bonnett of Womens Memoirs.com.** Matilda was our guest editor in our first issue and I hope you've invested in yourself by purchasing her excellent book on memoir writing, ***WRITING ALCHEMY***.

Matilda and Kendra ran a contest in 2014 for the best opening paragraphs to a memoir, and I must say their choices for the best opening paragraphs were excellent. Let me share a few with you here. Read them, think about them and ask yourself WHY? Why are these great beginnings to a memoir? As Matilda so rightly says:

You Don't Get a Second Chance at a First Impression!

"When I was young, my mother often reminded me that I didn't get a second chance at a first impression. And she assured me that first impressions mattered. It might all sound a little trite, but if you want to have the opportunity for more impressions, even as a writer, you need to get the first one right."

Matilda and Kendra received many wonderful entries. Below are the top place winners:

A GRAND PRIZE WINNER:

"The tan leather upholstery, embossed like a honeycomb, enveloped our family with its sweet familiar scent. I always sat on the right side of the Mercedes's back seat, behind my mother in the passenger seat. Whenever all four of us climbed into the car, whether to go to my grandparents' house, on a Sunday drive, or a long summer journey, I called the right side. My brother thought I preferred to look out of the window at things along the side of the road, but I held the true reason to myself. I had imagined, forever, that should the car, for whatever unknown and bizarre reason, split in half lengthwise, break apart along its axis and become two separate two-wheeled vehicles, I'd be with my mother. We'd leave the boys behind and she'd steer me toward the future."

A GOLD PRIZE WINNER:

"Light filters through the stained glass window, Jesus on the Cross illuminating the altar and flowers arranged there by my mother, an altar guild member. As the priest intones the Episcopal Eucharist, I squirm in my seat next to her. Perhaps to atone for my lapses, I force myself to sit still. I did not attend the stepfather's funeral, nor did I visit *him when he lay sick three months in a hospital bed. I have not explained; no one has asked. Mom directs me to hold the prayer book as she prays, and as she sings her beloved hymns I hold the hymnal just so, like I did as a child. I have never liked the way she moves her mouth when she prays or when she sings the high notes, righteous in her denial. I want to run."*

A SILVER PRIZE WINNER:

"I entered the world one Sunday afternoon in mid-February 1948, the firstborn child of an unwed fifteen-year-old. Her Catholic parents were surprised by my arrival. So, says my mother, was she. "

Thanks to Matilda Butler of Womens Memoirs for allowing me to share these with you. Read more contest winners on her website HERE:

http://womensmemoirs.com/memoir-writing-news/womensmemoirs-first-paragraph-contest-announcement-of-gold-winners/

(This article was originally published by Viga Boland in Memoirabilia Magazine, Issue #2, October 2015)

WHY WRITING MEMOIR MATTERS
By Viga Boland

http://www.vigaboland.com

If everything I've shared with you in "Don't Write Your MEmoir without ME!" and in all the advice and editorials presented in the last few pages, hasn't yet convinced you that writing memoir matters, then I urge you to get yourself a copy of

THE MEMOIR REVOLUTION
By JERRY WAXLER
http://www.jerrywaxler.com

Below is a book review I wrote of this amazing book and published in Memoirabilia Magazine #2 in May 2015. I was both blown away and inspired by what I read in Jerry's book. Apart from facilitating memoir writing, like me, Jerry devotes much of his reading time to memoirs by both traditionally published and self-published writers. His website abounds with essays and reviews of memoirs. So if I can't convince you of the nobility and need for writing memoirs, perhaps Jerry can. Here's what I think of "The Memoir Revolution" by Jerry Waxler:

"It's rare for me to pick up a book and not be able to put it down. I've come close a couple of times when reading a true crime story, but never when reading a book about writing memoirs. But that's what happened when I picked up MEMOIR REVOLUTION by Jerry Waxler. And before you say, "oh it's another book about how to write your memoir", let me assure you that isn't what kept me riveted for four non-stop hours.

What was it then? It was Jerry Waxler's undeniable passion for his subject: memoir writing. If you are postponing writing your memoir because that inner critic inside you insists no-one will want to read about your ordinary life, Jerry Waxler will have you thinking otherwise in no time. Waxler believes there's a revolution taking place in writing and it's all about writing what really matters, writing those stories that will help readers better understand mankind and all its differences in race, culture, color and religion. When ordinary, every day people share their truths, those differences shrink. And for the memoirists, as we write we too begin to better understand how our own pasts dictate our presents and impact our futures. This powerful revolution of understanding for both writers and readers rests in the pens and minds of those who choose to share their memories. Fiction is fine; it's a release, an escape, but often quickly forgotten. Memoirs, those true stories of pain, hardship, love lost and found, battles waged and won are timeless.

Jerry Waxler is a therapist, memoir workshop facilitator, an author and prolific book reviewer. His personal website and his Memory Writers Network site are a "must" visit, full of invaluable information of interest to memoir writers and memoir readers. The book reviews and essays are incredible, as are Waxler's writing prompts.

If you don't pick up a copy of MEMOIR REVOLUTION, you're missing out on one of the most motivational books ever. Thanks for reminding me Jerry Waxler why I write and read memoirs. 5 stars!"

*****

So what do you say? Are you ready to come join Jerry Waxler, me, and all the writers whose stories and book excerpts I present on the following pages in a "Memoir Revolution"?

Read on! What follows are memoirs written by people just like you who know that writing memoir matters!

STORIES, BOOK EXCERPTS

FEATURED in

MEMOIRABILIA

http://www.memoirabilia.ca

SOOTY

An Excerpt from the book
"Two Decades of Diapers"
by Barbara Studham

As a kid, I wasn't keen on schedules, but every Saturday would see me up and out by 7:00 am, cycling like crazy to the local farm to purchase fresh straw for my rabbit.

"Bring a bigger bag next time," the farmer would urge while watching me stuff handfuls into my school satchel.

"I will," I always promised then, throwing the bag over my shoulder, I would cycle as recklessly home, run to the back yard, and unload the straw.

"Look, Sooty, this is for you," I would squeal as he nervously backed away.

Sooty had belonged to a neighbour who no longer wanted the bother of his upkeep. "He comes with a hutch," she had explained to my mother, who sighed and shook her head.

"No thanks, Mrs. Pond. I don't need a rabbit," Mom had muttered then, nodding toward me, added, "I have enough trouble with this one."

"But, Mom, he's so beautiful!" I gasped. "Please can we have him, Mom? I promise to look after him!"

After several hours of hearing my pleading and empty promises, Mom finally relented and so I raced to my back yard where my neighbor was working in her yard.

"Mrs. Pond! Mrs. Pond!" I yelled over the fence, "Mom said—yes— I can have the rabbit!"

Her smile widened. "Here you go then," she said, picking Sooty up in his cage and handing it to me. "I've got a sack of straw in the garage. I'll get it for you."

As she passed the hutch over the fence and into my eager hands, I thought I would burst with excitement. I looked around for the perfect place to display him, like an award I had received for reaching the age of ten and therefore deserving of a rabbit. But, as I scanned the yard, I heard the living room window open and my Mom yell.

"He's your responsibility, now!"

"I know Mom," I called, having no idea what responsibility meant.

For the next year or so, I groomed and petted Sooty, changed his straw, and with every opportunity showed him off to the neighborhood kids who envied my having a rabbit with soft, shiny black fur, a bobbing tail, and sharp appealing eyes. I delighted in their arguing over who would hold him next, feeling much older than my years as I made them line up to take a turn. I truly loved Sooty and knew he loved me.

Then, one Saturday, my uncle came to visit. When he arrived, I was in the garden cleaning Sooty's hutch and feeding him fresh lettuce leaves I had stolen from my Dad's garden. Suddenly, I noticed my mom standing a way off watching me. She had recently complained over the cost of Sooty's upkeep so I intuitively sensed danger, but was surprised when she simply turned around and walked back inside the house. When convinced Sooty was clean and well fed, I gave him one last kiss, locked his cage, and headed off to play.

"Be back at one for lunch," my Mother shrieked from the kitchen window.

"I will Mom!" I yelled back, running as fast as my legs would take me to avoid being grabbed by the long-legged spiders inhabiting the high, green, privet hedge that surrounded our house. "I promise!"

So, at one o'clock I was back home, sitting at the table, innocently swinging my legs waiting for lunch to be served, but noticed the table was only set for one. Hearing my mother, sister, and uncle in the kitchen whispering and giggling, I called, "Isn't anyone else having lunch?"

"Nope, only you," called Mom, bringing in a large bowl of steaming stew and setting it down before me. "Eat up while it's hot."

After my busy morning, I was hungry and so tucked into the stew but, after only a few spoonful's, muttered, "It tastes funny." I glanced at my mom and uncle who were standing in the kitchen doorway smirking. I sensed something was up, but I was too afraid of my mom to refuse to finish my meal, so downed the whole bowl, and then ran back outside to play.

Later that evening when my uncle had left and I lay on my bed exhausted from play, my sister came to my room. "I have a secret to tell you," she murmured enticingly, and leaned in to whisper in my ear.

Startled by her words I jumped up, raced downstairs, and out to my rabbit's hutch, but Sooty was gone.

"Sooty, where are you?" I cried, frantically searching the garden, all the time calling his name. "Sooty, Sooty, where are you?" But, there was not a murmur, nor a squeak. I began to cry and ran back inside.

"Mom! Mom! Do you know where Sooty is?" I cried, hoping my sister's revelation was a lie.

But, when I ran into the kitchen, and saw my Mom expression, I knew it was true. Mom had asked my uncle to kill Sooty, skin him, and prepare him for the stew.

My heart died. "Mom, where is Sooty?" I whispered.

Staring defiantly, she smirked, "In your stomach."

© *Barbara Studham, 2014*

MY FIRST LOVE

By Heather Lamb

He was a Saskatchewan farm boy, born and bred. His name was Wilber. I know it's an old-fashioned name, but somehow it suited him. I fell in love with him the summer I turned eleven years old. He was the first boy I ever truly loved, besides Dad.

It was summer vacation and as we drove over the Kelfied hill, the last descent to the farm, I squinted in the bright July sunshine. I searched the serene countryside, laid out in patches of neatly planted crops. Off in the distance I could see the proud bright red of the barn, criss-crossed in braces of white. The neat white clapboard house stood in the farmyard.

"There's the farm!" I squealed, the air crackling with my excitement.

By the time we turned into the dusty driveway, flanked by an old rusty wagon wheel, I could barely contain my enthusiasm.

I sat twitching and bouncing as we visited my grandparents. Grandpa finally spoke and set me free.

"Well, Heather, do you want to go out to the barn? There's someone out there I want you to meet."

"Out in the barn?" I asked. "Is it the Larson girls or Shelley Rogers?"

"Nope. Come on, you'll see."

I raced across the yard, Grandpa following with his faithful dog, Laddie, at his side.

A beam of sunlight pierced the cool, foggy damp of the barn, motes of hay dust dancing in the rays. The smell of the animals mixed with manure and the fresh clean scent of the hay was the aroma of heaven to me. I squinted into the darkness, waiting for my eyes to adjust to the dim interior.

101

Then I saw him.

He sat in a small pile of hay at the foot of the ladder which led to the loft. His hair was coarse and the palest blond, almost white. It stood up in little spikes at the crown of his head. I noticed that his hair was rather thin. I could see the pink of his scalp, because he was so fair. His lashes were long and gorgeous, framing his lids in strands of the same pale hue. His eyes were the deepest, most soulful brown.

One look at him set my heart on fire. They say there is no such thing as love at first sight, but I fell for Wilber instantly. I was hopelessly and completely in love.

He raised his head and nodded in greeting. He grunted a terse 'hello', as I shyly approached him. I turned to Grandpa and waited to be introduced.

"This little guy stays out here in the old horse stall. He made a bed in the hay. He's really friendly, aren't you boy?"

I reached out my hand and ran it across his bristly head. He nodded and raised his slimy, flat pink nose to my hand and snuffed. He grunted again as I sunk to my knees and wrapped my arms around his chubby pink body.

"I'm going to name him Wilber," I said dreamily, as I scratched his coarse skin, causing him to stretch in delicious ecstasy. "It's a perfect name for a pig."

Grandpa explained that Wilber's mother had rejected him, chased him from the litter and slashed the tendons in his legs as he ran. He had nursed with another sow, but he was crippled. Now he just sat in the barn, dragging himself after Grandpa as he went about his chores.

My heart broke for the poor little guy as I heard the story. It further cemented my love for him. I spent every waking moment of our vacation at Wilber's side. In the first fledgling days of our romance, we were content sitting side by side; I scratched him until my fingers were almost raw from his bristly hair. He was in heaven as I brought him morsels from the slop pail or freshened his water from the tap.

He waited in his stall for me each morning. When I hauled the huge barn door open, sliding on its massive rusty rails, Wilber squealed with delight. He grunted noisily and shifted back and forth on his front hooves in a dance of anticipation. Then he dragged his rear end toward me across the time-worn wooden floor.

After those first blissful days, I wanted more for Wilber. One morning the idea came to me as in a vision. I moved behind Wilber, as his eyes followed me in adoration. I reached down and grasped his wiggly curly tail. Up, up, I hauled his meaty bottom, until his back toes brushed the floor of the barn. As if he understood what I was offering, his weakened legs began to shuffle. He leaned forward onto his strong front legs, and took his joyous first steps, me tugging his butt upward with all the feeble strength in my skinny eleven-year-old arms. His back toes dusted the floor. We were off!

I spent hours walking Wilber around the barn and out into the yard, my back breaking with the effort. The joy in Wilber as he snuffled in the grass or rooted his flat wet nose against the buildings made my aches and pains disappear. He snorted in the essences and aromas of the farm and relished in his freedom. I let him wander anywhere he chose to lead me.

"Heather!" hollered Grandma from the back door. "Get that pig out of my garden!"

I threw Grandma a beaming grin of delight; she watched aghast as Wilber happily munched on a row of carrots and waggled his ears for all he was worth. Mounds of dirt pushed aside by his curious snout patterned the tidy rows in Grandma's garden. The pea patch looked a bit sparser as well.

Wilber's legs grew stronger as the days flew by. At the close of our two-week vacation, he was walking shakily on his own. He lost his balance at times, his pudgy butt slamming to the ground. But now, as I ran to help him, he was able to haul himself to his feet. He tottered off, his tail swinging wildly in carefree circles.

It broke my heart to leave him.

"I'll never forget you Wilber," I crooned, as I kissed his rough head. "I'm so glad you'll have a happy life on the farm now."

I waved goodbye through my tears and as I looked back to him, Wilber lifted his head and snorted, grinning widely. I knew in my heart he would not forget me either.

In the fall of that year, the year of my first love, I received a letter from my Grandpa. I opened it eagerly, longing for news of Wilber's progress. A cheque fluttered from between the pages and fell to the floor. I picked it up and looked at it in confusion.

"Why is Grandpa sending me money? It's way past my birthday and it's not Christmas yet."

Mom read the letter.

"Grandpa took the pigs to market. This money is for you, because your pig was healthy enough to sell."

I cried buckets. I wailed and grieved, knowing Wilber's life was over. And it was all because of me. I was bitter and spitting mad at both Grandpa and the evil men at the slaughterhouse who had murdered my sweet darling Wilber.

Only one thought brought me a modicum of comfort.

"Oh Wilber, I hope you made it hard for those horrible men. I hope you broke free and made a run for it."

©Heather Lamb, 2015

RAGING HORMONES
By Billy Morgan

As a young man with raging hormones, imagine my frustration upon graduation when I secured a placement in a remote radar station where most of the resident airmen were already dating the few available village girls. My colleagues teased me mercilessly, constantly suggesting I take cold showers every time I sighed as a pretty girl passed by the windows of the station. But one Saturday afternoon when I was lining up to enter a cinema in Helston, near Land's End, I noticed a somewhat sickly looking girl with scabs around her eyes in front of us. My married airmen friend who knew how to talk to girls, somehow managed to get her to give him her phone number. Scabs or not, I was excited. I repeated her number to myself over and over throughout the movie, determined to give her a call. When I got back to base I saw my big chance of meeting a real live girl for the first time.

Unfortunately, the only phone on the camp was in the guard room and I did not fancy talking to a girl with two hefty military policemen hearing every word I said. I borrowed the camp bicycle and rode to the nearest transmitting tower. I climbed its vertical three hundred foot ladder to look for a bright red phone box. Spotting one about a mile and a half away, I descended the ladder and ran as fast as my legs would carry me. Huffing and puffing, I reached the phone box only to find it had been vandalized. My disappointment was great, but my desperation to get a date was greater.

Back I ran to the camp. Again I climbed the 300-foot tower. Shielding my eyes against the setting sun, I saw one about two miles away. Down the tower I scrambled, nearly twisting my ankle in my eagerness to reach the ground and get to that phone-box before dusk. But alas, my need was not to be realized as that phone box had also been vandalized. I wasn't about to climb the tower again so I gave up. Perhaps the Lord was looking after me that day. After all, who knows why that girl had scabs around her eyes!

©Billy Morgan, Mississauga, Ontario, Canada

WHEN CHICKS ARE SMARTER THAN HENS

*An Excerpt from the book, **"Learning to Love Myself"***
By Viga Boland
www.vigaboland.com

"Victoria, cool it honey."

Victoria stopped, frowned and made a face at Kim. Kim stuck out her tongue and put her nose back into her book. I replied to Victoria's question.

"Yes, I did look into the talent school, Victoria, but it's very expensive. I just don't know if we can afford it."

Victoria fixed me with her 'what Vicki wants, Vicki gets' look, the one that spelled I'd lost this argument. She'd first given me that look years back when she and I were having it out about what she wore to daycare. She'd wanted to wear only pretty dresses, and a different one every day. I'd wanted her to wear shorts and t-shirts, suitable for playing in sand pits and climbing monkey bars.

One morning we were having a screaming match over it and I bolted for the toilet with a sudden urgent need. She was right behind me and barged through the bathroom door before I could close it.

"I want to wear this today!" she demanded, showing me a brand new dress I'd just bought for her birthday.

"No way! That's for your birthday. And would you mind giving me some privacy please," I grimaced as I tried to hold back a pressing bowel movement.

"No!" she stormed and plunked herself down on the floor directly in front of me.

"No!" she said again as I exploded into the toilet. She went on ignoring my discomfort and embarrassment. "You see, mummy,

I've been thinking about this problem and I have a solution."

"Can your solution possibly wait till I'm off here Victoria? This is rather awkward."

"No!" she replied, determined that I would listen.

I gave up. "Okay, what is it?"

"Well, I can see your problem," she began.

"Oh, it's my problem is it?"

"Yes," Victoria replied with a wisdom beyond her years. "It's your problem because you want me to wear shorts and t-shirts to daycare, and I want to wear my pretty dresses. So we're always fighting about it. But..." She looked up at me, her beautiful brown eyes twinkling with pride, "but, here's my solution to your problem. How about one day I wear a dress and the next day I wear shorts. That way you get what you want and I get what I want."

"You mean a compromise?" I smiled, awed by how she'd thought this through. "But could you stick to that?" I asked.

"Yes! I promise. I will. What do you think?"

"I think I'd like you to let me get off this toilet while you get dressed or we're going to be late!"

"Okay," she jumped up brightly, but then stopped and fixed me with her fiercest Victoria look. "But did I give you the solution to your problem? And can I wear this dress today? I promise to wear shorts and T-Shirt tomorrow."

How could I argue with such logic from the mind of my child? It made perfect sense. I was proud of her for coming up with such a solution, and she stuck to her promise. She taught me a valuable lesson in parenting that day: let children resolve a contentious issue and they are more likely to follow through than when we demand they do what we say.

THE TEACHER'S HANDS
An Excerpt from the book,
"The Full Catastrophe"
by Karen Lee

Sometimes you remember the story, but not the significance, the memory but not the emotion. It lies in wait for that moment when you aren't expecting it. That's what happened to me. In September 1998, I went to Prague to conduct a training program. My usual co-facilitator wasn't free that week, so he recommended David, a consultant familiar with the programs we were running.

I met David in the hotel lobby, and we walked to a restaurant in old town Prague to discuss the project. Part way through dinner I could feel an uneasiness creep over me – something I couldn't put my finger on. The next morning, we met before the group arrived for the workshop, and David suggested an ice-breaker as a beginning to the day. Before I could stop myself, I answered him, "I'm not going to do that exercise. You can just think of something else."

For the next forty-five minutes, repeatedly criticized this perfectly reasonable man. I could see the growing alarm and dislike on his face. Halfway through that first morning, a cold fear came over me as I confessed to him, "I'm so sorry. Your hands remind me of someone, something that happened a long time ago."

This ordinary man, had my Teacher's hands. Fat and white, pudgy and doughy fingers. My Teacher's hands were sticking out of the sleeves of this otherwise normal man. Angrily, he turned away. He didn't want to talk with me, and, frankly, there was no good way to explain to a complete stranger that he had the same hands as a pedophile.

I'd never understood why I had an obsession for looking at men's hands. But that morning, something clicked into place. Here, thousands of miles from my childhood home, my Teacher had sprung up, out of the past, with no warning.

© Karen Lee, ***http://karenelee-author.com/index.html***

GOODBYE BATMAN
By Michael Gause

It was the spring of 1979, and junior high was just a couple months away. Where were we? Any small town in the south where kids torture bugs with firecrackers. Girls had started to look different this last year, and not just to us. Our toys were gathering dust on shelves and under beds. There was a fire in our blood, and no amount of clandestine porn or ice cold drink seemed to quench it. We weren't sure how different seventh grade would be, but we had heard stories. It was a sharp and shimmering landscape somewhere between the simplicity of childhood and the expectations of men. We talked a lot about it, asked questions, and tried not to show our fear to one another or to our friends. Whatever it was, it was coming, and we needed to be ready.

We'd seen it all on Sunday afternoon television, where mysterious men stood tall and kicked ass with honor. We'd seen our Bruce Lee, our Chuck Norris. We had seen Good Guys Wear Black from the hood of my father's Buick the summer before. Norris had given us a path, and we aimed to take it. Our old secret hideout was now used to store fishing poles and tackle. If you looked inside on the wall, you could still see where we used to hang our walkie-talkies. No, now it was time to learn to protect ourselves like men.

One day after school, without really talking about it, my buddy and I found ourselves making nunchucks out of old chair legs in his backyard. With an old baseball bat we spent half an hour smashing the hell out of an old school desk, the old-fashioned kind which was just a chair with a flat surface attached at a swooping angle to just under your ribs. We took two legs apiece and nailed a length of string into the end of them. Goodbye, Batman. So long, Spiderman. The time for superhero hopes was gone. Super powers hadn't stopped bullies since second grade, anyway. But these, these ancient sticks were going to keep the larger world from getting the best of us. We had watched the movies; we knew if you swung them fast enough, you could take on an army. An army. My friend found a block of wood his dad split last fall. He set it upright on a stump. I cocked the weapon under my arm. You will not take me. I shifted my footing. I am no longer a child. I swung hard. I will not be a victim in the world that waits.

In the blink of an eye, the stick bounced off the block as if made of rubber and hit me square in the head. I hit the ground, and a siren went off everywhere around us. Watching the clouds spinning overhead, I wondered if this was what growing up was like, wondered if this is what it's always like, a strange siren voice I now heard laughing, calling me out by name.

PEPPERELL LAKE
An Excerpt from the book,
"Alabama Blue"
by Toni K. Pacini

(You can listen to Toni reading this excerpt in Podcast #17 at MEMOIRABILIA)

Alabama summers brought sun and more sun, accompanied by suffocating degrees of humidity. We lived in Pepperell Mill Village, and Pepperell Lake was about a mile up the road. That mile seemed like ten on an especially vicious summer day. You'd think those of us born and raised there would become accustomed to the heat. No one ever seemed to. When my grandparents, and later my momma, had to go into the cotton mill during those scorcher days it was not uncommon for people to faint away, right there on the work floor.

Sometimes on one of those hot, airless days, Momma would walk with my sister and me to the lake so we could take a swim. My sister and I would start the walk jabbering about this and that. The farther we walked with that endless sun beating on our heads, the quieter we became. The asphalt along the highway would be steaming, buckling under the relentless summer heat. We felt like we were wilting and in danger of melting into the shimmering asphalt, oozing liquid into the earth.

Once we turned off the highway onto the dirt road that led to the lake, each step created a red dust cloud, encouraging us to hurry along to the cool water. The lake provided a great escape from the heat, and we'd laugh and play with wild abandon, energized by the cool relief. Although we were free and raucous, we respected the lake and her rules. We never swam out past the rope.

Every child from the village and surrounding areas had been taught since his or her first dip in Pepperell Lake to stay on the beach side of the rope that divided the lake into two parts. One half of the lake, the swimming section, was divided into three smaller parts. The larger section of the three made up the main swimming area, with an easy sloping embankment and a dirt bottom. I loved the way the wet earth squished between my toes.

The remainder of the swimming area held two square concrete pools. The larger for less experienced swimmers and a wading pool for the toddlers.

Momma never learned to swim. She'd sit on the edge of the wading pool with the other mothers, smoking cigarettes and drinking sweet tea while she dangled her slender legs in the water. The other half of the lake, the section beyond the rope and considered off limits, was left untended and was home to fish, birds, and snakes. The caretaker of the property frequently dragged the section used for swimming. He made sure no debris drifted into the recreational area where a snake might linger, camouflaged by a limb or log. Snakes are a part of life in the South. Near the water you are always on the lookout for water moccasins and rattlesnakes might show up pretty much anywhere.

One day while my sister and I were frolicking in the water, a horrible thing occurred. I will never forget that boy's screams. He played in the water with his friends, and they had been out precariously near the rope. Looking back, I wonder if they were out so far to escape the disapproving stares of the others at the lake that day.

The boy swam fast under the water, attempting to stay ahead of a friend who playfully gave chase, and when the child resurfaced, he did so directly under a moccasin. Water moccasins are not social critters. Their babies are born alive and immediately take off to fend for themselves. Moccasins are natural loners and will not go out of their way to attack. They will avoid humans whenever possible. But when that little boy accidentally crashed right into that moccasin, she did what came natural. She bit the intruder over and over again until he became quiet and still.

The real sadness that day, and the source of my sorrowful memory wasn't solely because a child had died. The real horror came from what I heard the grownups say only minutes after the dead boy's tiny, golden brown body, glistening with beads of water catching the day's sunlight, was removed from the lake. The grown-ups laughed, some genuine, some nervous and uncertain, but they laughed.

One man said, "No big loss; one less nigger to put up with."

In response a big, red-faced man laughed with a crude snort, and said, "Hell, I didn't even know snakes liked dark meat."

I learned that day that not all snakes are belly crawlers. The two-legged ones can sometimes be meaner than the ones who slither and hiss.

©Toni K. Pacini, *"Alabama Blue"*
http://www.toni-k-pacini.com/alabama-blue.html

BEFORE THE BOAT BEGAN TO SINK
By Nancy Gufstasen

*Originally published, October 2015, by **Imitation Fruit***
Republished & Podcast in March 2016, with permission on
Memoirabilia

Their plan was to build a boat using an eight-foot sheet of rusty tin that had blown off the chicken house during a hurricane. The brothers, twelve-year-old Jan and six-year-old Kurt, bent the tin in half lengthwise and nailed the ends around scrapped two-by-fours. They wedged boards in the middle to hold the sides in place and serve as seats. Then they sealed seams and holes with gooey black tar. Their paddles were warped fence posts, and they tossed two coffee cans in the boat to bail water just in case the tar failed.

They were intrepid adventurers—the Lewis and Clark of Alvin, Texas. Lured by a pond on Mr. McCauley's farm, they lugged the boat across their pasture, a sea of cockleburs and nettles that stuck in their bare feet and stung their legs below the cuffs of their rolled-up blue jeans. Shirtless and hatless, their shoulders and noses were sunburned and covered with freckles. They stopped occasionally to wipe sweat out of their eyes, pull a sticker from a foot or swat away mosquitoes.

When they finally reached the fence between their pasture and Mr. McCauley's, they licked their fingers to test the wind. It was blowing from the southwest, increasing the chance that the McCauley's Brahma bull wouldn't smell them. He was a huge gray bull with a black hump on his back, fiery eyes, saber-like horns and floppy ears. When he walked, an enormous dewlap swung from his neck. He was a mean son-of-a-gun known to charge and stomp intruders.

The boys forced the canoe under the fence, tin screeching against barbed wire. They eyeballed their destination, half a football field away in a Bermuda grass pasture: a shallow pond, where the bull and his harem drank and bathed. No cattle in sight, they continued their journey. By the time they wrestled the boat through the dense grass, they were wet with sweat and dragging their feet. The boys hefted the boat around senna bean trees and rushes that grew along the edge of the pond, disturbing red winged blackbirds that flew off in all directions like Roman candles. They launched their boat next to a floating clump of jelly filled with black-spotted frog eggs.

As they paddled into the murky world of snakes and turtles, Jan and Kurt grinned at each other, their noses crinkling into freckled washboards. The boat glided smoothly. Only a small amount of water trickled in at first. But by the time they reached the middle of the pond, the bottom of the boat was filling with water. They bailed wildly with the coffee cans as the tar gave way and water gushed in, but they could not stop the boat's descent into the pond's muddy bottom. Eye-to-eye with the dinosaur-like heads of snapping turtles, they used their paddles to keep them at bay. The boys struggled to help each other slip free of the mud that sucked at their legs, and they slithered like salamanders across the slimy water and crawled onto the grassy bank. Repulsed by the leaches they pulled off each other and exhausted from the effort of their ordeal, they lay on their backs and stared at buzzards circling in the cloudless blue sky.

Unperturbed by their failed boating venture, the boys decided to play dead and see if they could trick the buzzards into landing on them. They held as still as road kill, their arms and legs akimbo, their tongues lolling out the sides of their open mouths. They squinted their eyes and watched the buzzards through their lashes. The trick was working! The buzzards were circling lower and lower.

Trying not to move his lips, Jan whispered "Grab the legs of the first one that lands." Then they heard it—a sound like a jungle drumbeat in a Tarzan movie. No, it was more like pawing, like a water buffalo getting ready to charge the natives. When they heard the snort, they knew it was the bull!

They scrambled to their feet and sprinted for their lives, with pounding hooves drawing closer and closer. Reaching the fence, they threw themselves to the ground and squeezed under the bottom wire, bare chests scraping over burs and nettles. Kurt's jeans hooked on a barb and ripped as Jan pulled him free, just in the nick of time. The Brahma skidded to a stop. Enraged, he stomped and snorted, a cloud of insects rising around his hooves. When they reached a safe distance from the fence, the brothers turned one last time to watch steam rising from the nostrils of the still furious bull. Secure on their side of the fence, they grinned at each other like Cheetah.

This was not the last time Jan and Kurt would build something out of junk and try to make it float, nor was it the last time they would bail each other out of rising water. Through the years the brothers extricated each other from muddy situations, pulled off blood-suckers, warned each other when they spotted circling buzzards, and helped each other up after they had ripped their britches. They passed these virtues on to their sons and daughters.

Nowadays they sit around campfires with their children and grandchildren. They roast marshmallows and retell the stories of their youth—wonderful adventures that seem to grow in magical detail. They are told that they have excellent memories. So excellent, in fact, that they can even remember things that never happened. Through the rising sparks of fire, they eyeball each other and grin like Cheetah—that same little-boy grin they shared just before the boat began to sink.

©*Nancy Gustafson*

BLUE
A book excerpt from "Blue" by Deborah Holzel

(Listen to Deborah reading this excerpt in Podcast #15 at Memoirabiia)

I knew that something terrible was happening to me. Every cell in my body seemed to be frozen. I felt cold to my core, even in the 90 degree heat. I wore my sunglasses all the time, indoors and out, to hide the tears that leaked from my eyes without warning. On the rare occasions that I found myself alone in the house, I crawled into bed and cried loudly and with such intensity that broken blood vessels appeared around my eyes. No one seemed to notice.

I went to see a counselor at the Student Health Center. I did a brief survey of the room. It was a basic, institutional office with bare, pale green walls. The counselor was an older, grey-haired woman.

"My boyfriend and I broke up."

I couldn't think of anything else to say. I looked down at the carpet, which was beige and a little worn under her chair and mine.

I continued to stare at the floor through our second session. I thought that I should be feeling uncomfortable because of the prolonged silence, but I couldn't work up the energy. I wasn't feeling very much at all.

Halfway through our third session, she said "You really need to get over this boy, Deborah."

I left and never went back.

I stopped seeing the few friends I still had. I had nothing to talk about. Why inflict my company on anyone else? Even I couldn't stand to be with me.

I sleepwalked through the summer and fall. I acted in plays and went on a few dates. Then I came home and cried.

George continued to spend time with Linda.

At a party that December, I asked a mutual friend what was going on with them. I tried to sound casual but couldn't meet his eyes.

"They're in love," he told me point blank. "George is discovering Linda just the way he discovered you. You need to face that, Deborah."

I suddenly felt nauseous and couldn't reply. I turned and went out the door without my coat and walked the four blocks to my house without feeling the cold. I walked through the front door without acknowledging my parents in the living room and ran up the stairs to my third-floor bedroom. Then I collapsed on the bed and began to wail.

My mother had followed me up the stairs to find out what was wrong.

"George is in love with someone else." I was moaning and writhing on the bed.

"You were still hoping after all this time. . ."

She didn't know what to do. She held me close, but I continued to wail. Then she half-heartedly slapped me, probably because that's what you did with hysterical women in the movies. Then she held me again.

I eventually calmed down, and she went downstairs. I lay in my bed, unable to sleep, staring at the ceiling until the room became lighter. Then I pulled myself out of bed and went downstairs to the kitchen, made some toast and attempted to eat it. It tasted like sawdust.

My mother sat down at the table with me.

"David heard you last night and it scared him." David was my six-year-old brother.

After that I kept my feelings to myself. I certainly didn't want to frighten little children. I pulled myself together and went about the business of acting in plays and finishing college, living what appeared to be a productive life.

No one knew that I was dying.

©*Deborah Holzel, "Blue"*

https://www.amazon.com/Blue-Deborah-Holzel/dp/1523648422

KANGAROO RESCUE: SNOOPY
An Excerpt from *"Old McLarsen Had Some Farms"*
By Christine Larsen

(Listen to Christine read this excerpt in her wonderful Aussie accent in Podcast # at MEMOIRABILIA)

The night was not so dark at all. A near full moon bathed the open spaces in soft grey light, striped with long dark shadows from the gum trees. When the lights of the ute were on full beam and the spotlight pointed its invasive finger through the bush, the deepest shadows had felt ominous, threatening unknown dangers. But now, the abrupt absence of artificial light and noise, and the eternity of space and quiet, gave me a wonderful feeling of being alone—and yet not lonely. The silent void enchanted me, stars sharply piercing the velvety blackness above. I fancied the large moon beamed down benevolently on all Earth's creatures. How total the sounds of silence in that clean fresh air, fragrant with the scent of gum trees. The harsh bush of daylight was different in the shadows of night. Softer now, dressed in its nightwear. Had I ever felt smaller or more insignificant? I couldn't remember anything quite like—

"There's one! Quick. Spot to the left. No! Bloody further left! What's the matter with you? Bloody asleep or something?"

The harsh words, and sudden roar of the engine as Sam started it, jolted me out of my reverie. A sideways lurch of the ute made me slide helplessly and heavily against him. Luckily he was anticipating this and had already braced himself and tightened his grip on the wheel. As my eyes refocused and sharpened from their dreamy state, the cause of the shouting—and the sudden forward thrust of the clamorous motor—was immediately apparent.

"Will you just look at that Boomer? Bloody huge!" Barry grunted, as he swerved around a soft looking patch of sandy soil. He knew this was most likely covering a tangle of rabbit burrows; the resulting collapse could cause serious bogging of the vehicle, at the least.

The 'old man' kangaroo <u>was</u> huge alright—magnificent, actually —in full flight ahead of us now, after our abrupt change of direction. He sailed through the air like a gust of wind, sinking back down to the dusty earth for another mighty spring, then gathering and soaring—again and again. Weaving in and out of the scrub and the light, he was gracefully fluid in his flight from danger. Out again into an open expanse, his muscles rippling, long legs rhythmically stretching then bunching, stretching, bunching; head constantly turning, seeking escape. Suddenly he found his goal—a narrow, well-flattened path into dense scrub. Shots rang out. Close. Breathtakingly close to hitting the fleet-footed target, but sympathetic trees deflected the whining bullets. He'd found elusive escape and shelter from these crass intruders into his world. There were curses from the men, and quiet inward joy from me, as he escaped. As the ute slewed around, the hunters were left with frustration as their only reward.

Following the chase and brutal affront to that 'old man' kangaroo's dignity, my certainty about the adventure I had somewhat romantically pictured, was crumbling fast. I understood why the men were so upset. The increasing numbers of kangaroos were creating fierce competition for precious fodder. The damage and subsequent expense 'roos caused to fencing had reached alarming levels. I could even, reluctantly, accept shooting by good marksmen as being a humane choice, compared to the unimaginably slow and painful death by poisoning. And yet, none of these perfectly reasonable arguments could diminish the growing knot of guilt and unhappiness in the pit of my stomach.

I tried to keep up a good front. After all, we were guests, and the men were doing what farmers have had to do since the first dirt was turned, and the first paddock fenced. They were protecting what was theirs. I gradually became a whole lot quieter, as I wished desperately no more hungry intruders would be found on this hunt. I wished in vain. The worst was still to come.

They shot ten kangaroos that night. Some were dropped in full flight; others as they began to turn away from the dazzling brightness of the pitiless spotlight. Most were dispatched with a single shot, and none were left to suffer. This questionable kindness offered little comfort to me or the 'roos—and the destruction continued. The last victim was a gentle-faced grey doe, mesmerised by the alien spotlight, her soft stricken eyes stretched wide in confusion and terror. She offered a perfect target. After she had fallen, we could all see movement still continuing within her pouch. Overwhelming sickness engulfed me, rapidly transforming into red-hot rage, as one of the men pulled a joey from her lifeless body.

Guest or not, I couldn't control myself any longer. My fury boiled over and I exploded out of the cab, physically and verbally. I don't remember my words, but the feeling of outrage is with me still. I snatched the baby from him and bundled the confusion of legs and tail into my jumper, clutching this newly orphaned joey close to my heaving chest. It was a confronting moment.

It was unimaginable this shivering, woebegone, skeletal creature— wearing only the lightest covering of fur—would survive the stack of odds against him. But nothing was going to stop my Snoopy from steadily growing into a big Red Kangaroo, taller than most humans, but always and ever, a gentle giant. In his early growth, he would melt at the sound of my voice, and the touch of my hands. In Snoopy's eyes, we were mother and son. Out of tragedy grew the triumph of his survival.

©Christine Larsen, "Old McLarsen had some Farms"

https://cdstoryteller.com/tag/christine-larsen/

TWISTING at the CYO DANCE
An excerpt from the book, *"The Ladies of Loretto"*
by Viga Boland

I'm overjoyed. I cannot believe my father is letting me go to the CYO dance. Betty and I hug each other and jump around excitedly in front of him. He dismisses us with a wave of his hand telling my mom what silly schoolgirls we are. Mom reminds him we're just normal 16-year-olds and it's time for me to get out a bit.

After school on Friday, I spend hours going through my closet and drawers looking for something nice to wear. Everything I put on looks horrible, stupid! I'm so frustrated. I settle on a form-fitting dark blue winter skirt that comes down to mid-calf. It has a little bow at the back where there's a small split to allow me to walk. It's the trendiest skirt I have and all the girls on American Bandstand are wearing them. Mom bought it for me with the few dollars she had tucked away for herself.

When Betty arrives to pick me up, I want to die. She's wearing a beautiful powder blue dress with a big crinoline underneath, the other most popular style on Bandstand. It fits snugly on her petite waist before fanning out. Her hair is teased. She looks like Sandra Dee in "Gidget". My hair is teased too but I look like Sam Jaffe on Ben Casey.

"What a small waist you have Betty," says my father with admiration. He looks at me and laughs. "You need to eat fewer cream buns," he continues, pointing to my tummy protruding in the slightly tight skirt.

"And you need to stop buying them," my mother snaps back at him. "Heidi and Betty have different builds, that's all. Now let them go. Betty's father is waiting in the car."

I'm so nervous when we arrive at the church hall. The lighting is dim. I'm almost grateful for that. I'm not sure I want any of these guys seeing how ugly I am next to Betty. As my eyes adjust, I see lots of boys lined up on one side of the hall and we girls are lined up on the opposite side. The music starts but no-one dances. The girls are hugga-mugga discussing which guys are cute and who they hope will ask them to dance. The boys seem to be doing the same. Many of them are looking towards Betty. I'm standing near her, hoping one of them might be looking at me too. But without my glasses, I can't really see who's looking at whom.

As it turns out, I don't have to worry. No-one asks me to dance all evening. Betty is asked time and again. Some of the girls already have boyfriends in the group so they get to dance too. I stand there becoming more and more despondent. This isn't like American Bandstand at all where even the plain girls dance.

"Hey Heidi! Are you going to stand there all evening?"

It's Theresa, another one of my Polish friends from grade school days. We're in different classes at Loretto. She's much prettier than I am...most of the girls are...but she's super friendly. She has been dancing with her boyfriend but he had to leave.

"Well, what choice do I have," I respond. I'm ready to go home. "Who am I supposed to dance with when no-one asks me?"

"Dance with me!" Theresa says cheerfully. "Julian had to leave and I won't dance with any boy but him. But I can dance with a girl. Come on."

Theresa grabs my hand and drags me protesting onto the dance floor. I feel totally ridiculous dancing with a girl, but when 'The Peppermint Twist' comes on, I figure 'what the hell' and start to twist all out.

Through a blurry haze, I see both girls and guys twisting around the room, but in my immediate vicinity, a handful have stopped and are clapping to the music as Theresa and I give it all we've got. I'm enjoying the attention. I'm good at twisting and I know it. I add some up and down to the round and round when suddenly I hear and feel RIP! The zipper in my skirt splits and my skirt is sliding down. At the same time, the open seam at the back pops the bow and starts coming apart. I'm mortified. I run from the room to the girls washroom, with both Theresa and Betty crashing through the door behind me.

"Oh my God," cries Theresa looking at the back of my skirt. "What are you going to do? Betty, do you have a safety pin?"

Betty nods "no" but says she'll go back out and ask around. She comes back with two pins a few minutes later and my two friends do what they can to make the skirt wearable. But it's too late for me. The night has been spoiled. I sit on a bench in a far corner of the room watching everyone else dancing and wishing Betty's father would arrive to take us home.

"You're really good at the twist," says a boy's voice beside me. "Why did you dash off like that? I wanted to ask you for a dance."

I look at him in shock. A guy wanted to ask me to dance? As my eyes start to focus on him, I can see why he would ask me: he has a nice smile but big red pimples on his forehead and cheeks. Guess he's a wallflower too.

"So do you want to dance?" He persists.

"I can't. My skirt might fall down."

Perplexed, he looks at me then starts to wander off saying, "Well there's an excuse no-one's given me before!"

©Viga Boland, 2015. *"The Ladies of Loretto"*

http://www.vigaboland.com

GLORY

By Nancy Gustafson

An aide wheels my mother down the hospital hallway to the therapy gym. I walk beside, holding her hand. An exception is made—I get to observe the session because Mom refuses to go without me.

The room is painted gray, fluorescent lit. Through the only window, the roiling of rain clouds add to the dismal atmosphere. Six patients in wheelchairs form a circle. The youngest is 87 years old; the oldest, my mother, is 94. Their postures speak for them—nobody wants to be here. Some of them have medicine bags hanging from poles, measured doses flowing through IVs into their veins. Most of them have plastic oxygen tubes in their noses. One woman's back is so curved that she can barely raise her head. One man has no legs; another has a withered arm, his hand clutched in a fist.

The therapist moves to the hub of the circle. He is a bright cheerleader attempting to enthuse a reluctant audience. He guides them in warm-up exercises. Swollen ankles grind out orbs. Trembling hands lift one-pound weights. In five minutes they are exhausted. In rests between sets of exercises, the cheerleader encourages memories. They remember fifteen-cents-a-gallon gasoline, sleeping on pallets at grandma's house, pear pie baked in a woodstove.

Large ping pong paddles are passed out. Some patients grumble. This silly game is the last thing they want to do. The cheerleader tosses a spongy ball into play, aiming it at individual patients. When it is her turn, Mom hits it. She hits it again and again. Her eyes sparkle.

The man without legs becomes a drill sergeant. "Come on men, we can't let a woman best us."

They try harder. The cheerleader is happy. Mom licks her lips—the competition is on and she seldom loses one. Chuckles ripple around the circle.

When the session is over, while the paddles are collected and equipment is stored, memories commence. Your first car? A jalopy that needed constant repairs. Your first date? Got my first suit; didn't grow into it until after graduation. Favorite meals? Fried round steak with mashed potatoes and gravy—makes me hungry just to think about it! And then they remember deeper hungers: loved ones lost, buddies killed in war—Corregidor! A woman with no teeth mutters in a wheezy voice, "While you boys were having fun Over There, I raised four kids by myself." Heads nod, her essential work acknowledged.

A shaft of sunlight streaks through dark clouds. The room glows golden with the bond they formed today, golden with hope for tomorrow's session, golden with their glory. Backs are straighter, heads higher, they smile and high-five each other. But time is up and aides wheel their patients, these monuments to the greatest generation, out the door and down the hallway.

Mom is the last to leave the therapy gym. She reaches for my hand and whispers, "I was the best one."

©*Nancy Gustafson*

(Originally published in Memoirabilia Magazine #5, October 2015)

AFRICAN REBIRTH
By Melissa Lamb

I am sitting here, in my home, on my bed with all my pillows and my blankets, with my TV on, my laptop running, cell phone charging. I have running water at the twist of a tap, a hot shower if I desire, a toilet and a seat. I even have soft cushy toilet paper. The bathroom cabinet is stocked with deodorant, tampons, pads, make up, cleaning supplies. Lights turn on, and almost always get left on. I'm listening to my children talk about how bored they are at this very moment, how there is nothing on TV, no video games to play. And I am sad. I am sad because I think about all the beautiful, wonderful people I met on my last journey and how little they have and how very happy they are.

I left Canada angry and sad at my life and the not so nice turns it had taken. My beautiful marriage had fallen apart and all I had were a few things and my children. I was angry at so many things, which now upon reflection, are trivial, minute, moot even. I struggled everyday to get out of bed, to function, just because I was so angry. I hated that I had cable TV but could never find anything on to watch; that there was food in my cupboards but nothing I wanted to eat. I left desperately wanting to just clear my head, to erase all the bad things. I wasn't running from anything, I just need a change of pace, of scenery. And I came back at peace.

I am humbled sitting here, in awe of the women over there and the things they accomplish in a day, their daily struggles. I am in awe of the men who so desperately want to take care of the children they love so dearly but can't, because their wives died or were murdered. And now it is their job to look after the children and there simply isn't enough work to be found, no government check to be delivered each month.

I am crying remembering how happy the children were to run around and chase a tire rim with a stick, or throw around a half inflated ball. I am crying remembering how happy the young women and children were to know I had brought sanitary pads for them and they, for the time being, no longer had to use tissue paper, old socks, ripped up pieces of foam from their mattresses.

I realize now, that while I may sponsor a beautiful little boy there, and he may be the one that is in need, that it was I, not my little boy there, that needed saving. I am reminded that the little things we take for granted are the treasures some people will never even know. Being with those children made me realize that it's not the quantity but the quality that matters...not how many big or costly things you have but the people with whom you surround yourself. What matters is the attitude you adopt and wake up with every single day: a smile, a handshake, really can go a long way. Every morning you are given another day to tell those you love how much they mean to you, to extend your hand to those in need, to hold open the door for someone, to greet someone, to smile at someone.

I may not have been born African. But my heart beats African, and I bleed African. And I cry African.

Africa, Kisii, Safe Haven, and all the people in it, changed me.

Mimi ni kushukuru milele na atakupenda daima

To Bismark, I thank you for your smile. Your beautiful smile is what brought me to Africa. Your laugh brought me back to life.

Mimi nakupenda milele Bismark.

Asante Sana

© Melissa Lamb, 2012

Originally published in Memoirablilia Magazine #5, October 2015

I'LL ALWAYS HAVE PARIS

By Maureen McMorrow

My students had been warned. "Do not go out alone. Do not miss curfew."

The narrow street was already dark and clogged with motorcycles. There was something very wrong with this picture. This comfy haven for the rich and snobbish, the 17th arrondissement, had turned into a hood. Goodness sakes, it hadn't been that long...well, thirty-five years. But still.

In those days, I was young, lonely and scared when I arrived at 25 rue Cabonel in Paris. The building was terribly grand. My destination? The deuxième étage. An au pair girl's dream, according to the notice at Alliances Françaises: an older couple, a daughter in her twenties, a grandson of eight, and no babysitting.

Madame Benoit was a grand dame with white hair, pearls, silk blouse and wool skirt below the knee. She couldn't have been as old as she seemed. After all, her daughter was only in her mid twenties. However, she appeared fragile...until she spoke. Imperious comes to mind. I blanched as she issued the first of many edicts:

"If you agree, you cannot leave before time. My mother is ill and I will not be inconvenienced by the help coming and going." This was followed by "only one bath a week, only breakfast and dinner included, no friends in my room and cleaning the whole apartment every day." She paused, took a much needed breath. "Except Sundays, of course, when we are "en famille" and you are not."

I hoped that I had understood all that she had said. My French was perfunctory at best, her English apparently non-existent. "Ah, oui Madame. Don't worry."

On the back stairs we climbed to the eighth floor slowly, me dragging my worldly goods and she in her sturdy oxfords. Were her knees creaking? Perhaps it was the staircase. So this was it, what live-in domestics called home: a single bed, a dresser, a cold water tap. Not much, but all mine. A toilet? Oh, yes, but in the hallway. Well, not right out in the hallway, it was more like a closet. This was called a Turkish toilet. Whether the Turks were to blame is moot, but that was its name. Two metal footprints with a drain in the middle. Not only was the Turkish toilet a challenge, it was for all tenants, regardless of gender.

And so began my life with the family Benoit. Monsieur was quiet and kind, the daughter dour, the grandson a whiny eight year old. But he wasn't

my problem. I was my own problem. Already I was working in the shadow of my predecessor, Gerda. She had returned to Germany. Madame was her greatest fan.

"What a marvelous girl, so efficient, so gracious. Try to follow her example."

The harder I tried, the clumsier I got. First, a cracked candlestick. A little glue hid that indiscretion. Not so easily solved, the ceramic handle of the toilet brush broken in two. Madame was actually distraught.

"Oh, là là! A family heirloom. It cannot be replaced. Gerda would never treat me like this! I will take money from your wages."

I hung my head in shame. But the worst was yet to come. Every day I washed the bathroom floor after I had picked up the wet towels and returned them to the towel rack as instructed.

Madame had left the high overhead window ajar. I scrubbed enthusiastically, lost in thought. Wham! The wind had slammed the window shut, cracking it right down the middle. Well, what could I do? I was an innocent bystander. Madame Benoit didn't see it that way. She was furious.

"You broke my window!"

In my still halting French, I protested as vehemently as I could. "No, Madame, it wasn't my fault."

She was relentless. "You're a liar. You hit the window."

By now I was crying but angry. "I AM NOT A LIAR."

"Mais, oui, and I'm taking it out of your wages."

Soon the wages would be non-existent. What could I do? I hung my head and cleaned up the mess. Murphy's law continued to follow me everywhere; if something could go wrong, it did. One day I was sweaty and hot and wanted a bath desperately. Alas, I had already had my weekly ration. Contrary to my timid character, I decided to take my chances. Madame was at the market and I knew she'd be quite a while. I was wrong. I was splashing away, singing a happy tune when I heard pounding on the door.

"What are you doing? Why is the door locked?"

I was speechless.

"I demand an answer!"

I managed a little squeak: "I just had to have a bath, Madame. I just had to."

She was beyond rage. "Get out. How dare you? Gerda would never have done such a thing."

I was mortified as she railed at me and once again mourned the departure of the beloved fraulein. I don't recall ever having a bath in the apartment again.

One day I was heating water on a Bunsen burner for a sponge bath in my room. It was fairly windy and the French doors were open. I slipped out into the hallway for a moment. Bam! The door was locked. There I was, in a thin housecoat, commando and wearing clogs. I panicked. Thundering down the stairs, I reached the door of the concierge, practically keening.

"Du feu! Du feu! Help!"

"Keep calm , Mademoiselle. My son will help you."

But they had no extra key and I begged them not to tell Madame. Nothing would have it but that the young man would enter the room beside mine and leap from balcony to balcony. Fortunately, all went well. Another close call.

You may wonder why Madame Benoit didn't just send me packing. Well, she had other things on her mind. So did I the day she left me in charge of the oven. I was to turn off the roast in an hour. I was so busy cleaning and knocking things over, I completely forgot. In the meantime, Madame's nice daughter arrived. She was so kind and lovely.

"Don't worry. I'll say it was my fault."

I knew I was doomed once again. When Madame saw the pitiful, shriveled roast, she went into a rage. Chloe insisted that it was her fault. Madame was having none of it. Out went the roast, away went my wages.

It may seem as if nothing more could go wrong. I thought not too. I was trying to be so perfect and Gerda-like. One day at lunch, I was about to bring in the salad at the end of the meal, as is the custom in France. Madame heard the clicking of the salad servers as I mixed it with the dressing. She came flying down the hallway, seething

"What do you think you are doing? It's too soon. You've ruined the salad." Timing is everything. Things went from bad to worse. I could do nothing to please her. I couldn't get to sleep at night until dawn sometimes. I was so afraid not to wake up on time that I put coins in a pot with my alarm clock to make as much racket as possible. One morning, even that didn't work. In my dream I could hear a pounding that just wouldn't go away. I finally came to. There was Madame Benoit standing at my door. I thought my heart would stop. She was stone-faced.

"Get dressed immediately and come downstairs."

I knew I couldn't go on, in spite of my promise. I looked up nervous breakdown in the dictionary, went downstairs and told Madame I thought I was having one. I didn't know what to expect. To my surprise, she wasn't scathing or angry or critical.

"This is serious, Mademoiselle. You must take care of yourself. I will find someone else."

No doubt that was preferable to dealing with an emotionally unhinged foreigner. I couldn't believe it. I was free.

As it turned out, I would allow the bullies to win over and over again in my life. But at least I was free of 25 rue Cabonel, free of Madame Benoit and free of Gerda.

THE NORTH TO ALASKA ADVENTURE
By Lois Paige Simenson
http://loispaigesimenson.com

After living in Alaska for a few decades, it's hard to pin down just one or two adventures. Heck, stepping off your front porch to a startled moose is an adventure; or driving down the Glenn Highway in a raging blizzard. But then I did that in Montana. What I didn't do in Montana was slip and fall on a glacier sliding toward a crevasse, never to be heard from again. Obviously I didn't fall in.

I've been reflecting on my arrival to this odd and glorious place. I was in a honeymoon period upon arrival in Alaska; a bizarre time when everything seemed magical and foreign. Scotty had beamed me to another planet--only this one had people, cars, wild animals, and cows. White dominates the landscape most of the year. Once I had settled in, I felt I'd mastered something when I would arrive at my destination without slamming my car into a moose or a pissed-off driver with a truckload of guns.

Before leaving Montana, I wondered if I was moving to a cultural wasteland. I couldn't google in 1983. Will there be theatre, movies, entertainment? Will I be able to buy clothes or will I have to mail-order them from Sears? After all, having lived in Montana all my life where cows are the landscape, I had no clue. I needed reassurance so I called the guy in charge of moving us to Alaska.

"Do you have dairy products up there? I hear Alaska has no cows," I said to the travel guy.

Silence on the phone. Then, "Yes...we have cows here."

"Really—but do you have spices? I hear you can't get spices in Alaska."

Another silence. "Yeah. We have spices. You can even buy them at the grocery store."

I heard muffled laughter. "Oh good, grocery stores—so I don't have to stock up on anything to bring with me?"

"No ma'am. But don't bring meat. You can shoot it here." This time silence on my end.

I ambled to the spice store and stocked up anyway. You never know when you'll need a caraway seed. I still possess an antique jar of cinnamon from 1983. I need a chisel to get the cinnamon out. It's not that I didn't believe the travel guy: I was freaked about moving to the subarctic.

I then set out to buy my Alaska car. I spotted a TV ad that said the 'official car of Santa Claus' was the Toyota Tercel four-wheel-drive deluxe wagon. The car traversed rugged mountain ranges and plowed through white-outs like a blitzkrieg tank. I had to have that car. I didn't know if I would be trekking steep terrain to go to work in Anchorage. Best be prepared. We bought one.

The hard part was handing the keys of my precious new Toyota to a toothless greasy guy on the Port of Tacoma dock, who promised my car would be safely barged to Anchorage. Peering out the back window as the taxi rolled from the dock, I hoped I'd see my car again. It's not that I didn't trust the guy. I was freaked about moving to Alaska.

I flew from Seattle to Anchorage in November, sitting on the right for the best view. Gazing on the endless mosaic of bleached rose mountains, sapphire glaciers and turquoise ocean for the first time is indescribable. My nose flattened on the window, I gawked at the ceaseless alpenglow, windswept peaks, and jagged crevasses for the duration of the flight. I stayed transfixed, like seeing Mars for the first time. When we landed, my nose was red as Rudolph's from mashing it against the glass.

I picked up my official car of Santa Claus on a crisp morning at the Port of Anchorage. Once I recovered from the shock of what I paid the taxi driver, I approached what I thought was my Toyota in the weak morning light. Why was it pink? What happened on that barge on the stormy winter seas? A closer inspection revealed it was still red under the inch of hoar frost that concealed the color. Thank goodness it arrived in one piece. I stared at it, envisioning the wintry, thundering seas it survived to reach this alien planet.

Not only can I now buy spices in Alaska, I can mosey to Nordstrom for a designer dress to go with my Sorels; see Elton John at the Sully Arena, or Brian Regan at the Performing Arts Center. I can even buy a flat-panel TV. These things fly or sail from Seattle to Anchorage. When gas is cheap, they're trucked through Canada on The Alaska Highway. We may be far from mainstream America, but we aren't primitive, as the reality shows lead one to believe.

No, I can't drive from state to state in a heartbeat, the way I could in the Lower 48. It takes many heartbeats to drive to the nearest states—Washington or Montana—but I don't care. That's why God invented jets.

I've not regretted moving up to the Land of the Midnight Sun. Ever. Not one. Single. Moment. Ever. Not one. Single. Moment.

THE RED and BLACK BOA
By Viga Boland

The red and black boa startled me. I gasped in surprise. It was perfect, exactly what I was looking for...just what I needed for Samantha's costume. But who had put the boa in this old basement trunk? My mother? When would she have worn it? And why?

Though she'd often dreamed of it, I knew mom had never been on stage, but this was just the kind of thing a dancer or performer would wear. I closed my eyes envisioning her dancing around beneath red and green spotlights, tossing her golden hair and smiling becomingly. She was singing too. Her rich, melodious voice rang out across the theatre. The audience was mesmerized and she knew it. She was in her element, confident, beautiful, happy. The people had come to see her and she was giving them everything she had.

I opened my eyes again as the vision faded. As nice as it was, I knew it had never happened. I picked up the soft boa. Little red and black feathers loosened and floated gently down onto the dirty concrete basement floor. The boa was old. The more I touched it, the more feathers dislodged themselves. It most definitely hadn't been my grandmother's either. She was long dead and had never left Poland. But mom had. When WW2 ended, dad had brought her and me, just a baby, to Australia to begin a new life. According to dad, Australia would be a land of milk and honey. But for mom, the new world and her new life with a husband she didn't love, and a baby she never wanted, was anything but milk and honey.

Mom had loved to dance. She was a natural, with rhythm in every part of her body. But after she married dad, her movements became stiff, unnatural, her steps careful for fear of stepping on dad's toes or making a wrong move. She had loved to sing too but as the years went by the music went out of her heart and she rarely sang at all.

As she drew closer to her last days on earth, mom would tune into AM 740 and her eyes would light up when Nat King Cole came on and reminded her to "SMILE".

Smile though your heart is aching
Smile even though it's breaking.

When there are clouds in the sky you'll get by.
If you smile through your pain and sorrow
Smile and maybe tomorrow
You'll see the sun come shining through For you.
Light up your face with gladness,
Hide every trace of sadness.
Although a tear may be ever so near
That's the time you must keep on trying
Smile, what's the use of crying.
You'll find that life is still worthwhile-
If you just smile.

©*John Turner and Geoffrey Parsons*

She knew all about smiling: she'd been practising smiling since the first time Dad slapped her face when she was 18 and told her to smile when he was talking to her. She smiled when he commanded her to kneel down and kiss his little finger. She had thought he was kidding so she smiled, even laughed. But he wasn't kidding. He wiped the smile off her face with a kick in her swollen pregnant belly. She smiled when she served him the dinner she'd taken hours to prepare and he spat it at her asking what kind of garbage was she feeding him? She smiled as he took her paychecks and gave her a $1 a week allowance for being a good wife. And she even smiled when he called her a filthy whore and a stupid bitch with nothing between her ears. Only a smile and complete subservience was acceptable behavior.

I remembered all that now as I fingered the red and black feather boa, and wondered yet again how it had ended up in that trunk. It had to have been mom's but why did she have it? When did she buy it and why? Slowly, it came to me. After dad had passed away, mom started to live...never quite the way she wanted to since, after all, she was now far too old for dancing and singing on a stage. But at last she was free to go where she wanted and spend what she wanted. No more $1, $5, or $10 allowances generously doled out to her by the man who had ruled her life and controlled the purse strings for over fifty years.

Her old friends from the factory started urging her to come out with them. She was hesitant at first, but after a few trips to the local casino, coupled with lunch and shopping, she started smiling again. These were happy smiles, coming from her heart, smiles that arose from being able to indulge in the simple pleasures all other women took for granted. For the first time in over fifty years, she was truly enjoying herself.

She'd come home from a week away with bags of "stuff" that she'd purchased, not because she or any of us needed it, but just because she liked it and thought we might too. This week it was a ceramic doll for my adult daughter who'd long ago stopped collecting ceramic dolls. Next time it was an infant's crocheted cap and scarf, way too small for her 7-year-old great grand-daughter.

Another time, she carted home two sets of satin sheets for her own bed: they ended up being too slippery to sleep on especially once the chemo treatments started. Every shopping trip resulted in another pair of shoes that were pretty but pinched her swollen feet, or a pair of slacks that looked exactly like the ones she'd purchased on a previous trip. The elasticized waistbands on those had been too tight, later too loose; the legs too long for her 4'10" frame. She'd spend a week cutting and hemming the slacks by hand, her eyes blurry with cataracts, while she simultaneously watched old videos with Jeanette McDonald or Jane Powell or Carmen Miranda singing and dancing on the big screen. And she'd smile, living the life she had so wanted through these beautiful women of film.

The red and black boa. Yes. That was it. Mom had bought that for Victoria, my younger daughter, the one who did grow up to become the singer/dancer mom so wanted to be. She had thought Victoria might be able to use it in one of her shows, and even if she couldn't, well it was pretty, wasn't it? And besides, now, with him gone, she could buy whatever she wanted. So why not! There was no-one to tell her it was useless or ask her why on earth she'd want this or that silly thing. It was pretty and she liked it. That was all that mattered. That, and the fact that it made her smile.

I put the boa back in the trunk and closed the lid. I'd have to find something else to use for that costume. Even though mom was gone, I wasn't ready to see something "useless" that had brought a smile to her face used frivolously

What was useless about something that made a mother smile? That red and black feather boa was priceless.

©Viga Boland, 2014 *http://www.vigaboland.com*

MEMOIR BOOK REVIEWS
By Viga Boland
(Includes Memoirs &
Books on Memoir Writing)

The Final Word: What NOT TO DO
When Writing Memoir

Recommended Reading & Site Seeing

About the Author

"If you want to write memoir, READ
Memoir!"

(Viga Boland)

I AM WOMAN

A memoir by Daliah Husu
http://www.daliahhusu.com

For me, as a reader, there's nothing more satisfying than picking up a book that I just can't put down. That usually only happens if the book is a thriller or a mystery written by a very skilled writer. It rarely happens when I read a memoir. So what a treat to pick up Daliah Husu's **I am Woman** and find myself turning pages at "thriller speed." Not that **I am Woman** is a thriller, but for someone who is relatively unfamiliar with, and curious about what it is like to be born male and, and as an adult, transition fully into a female, I was enthralled by what Daliah Husu shared about her life. What was even better was that she has the skill to write a memoir as if she were writing fiction. I haven't found that talent with many memoirists. I had to pinch myself a few times to realize I was reading a true story.

A lot happens to Daliah in **I am Woman**. After Daliah is born, as a boy, into Dominican poverty, his birth mother leaves Daliah to be raised by a grandmother, only to summon him some years later to live in comparative wealth in the US. But after a divorce a few years later, as he's constantly getting into trouble, his mother sends him back to an upper crust Dominican boarding school. As Dalia grows, the many moves from place to place, and eventually from job to job once back in the US, parallel the inner transition from male to female. Keeping nothing back, Daliah Husu shares it all: dancing in gay bars, snorting cocaine, holding top-level management jobs, being arrested for prostitution and more. I am Woman discloses everything openly, honestly and emotionally. Daliah simultaneously loves and hates her life, looking for love of herself and others in all the wrong places, fighting internal and external demons all the way, yet never feeling sorry for herself. As a result, she earns the reader's full respect.

The most satisfying memoirs are those that relate a story of overcoming struggles and finding oneself in the process. Even more satisfying are those where, by the end of the journey, protagonists are, at last, at peace with themselves. They have come to love the beautiful person inside. In **I am Woman**, Dalia Husu emerges a multiple winner: she finds peace, learns to love herself, meets a loving soulmate and partner, and discovers her talent as a writer. She also earns a new fan: me. I look forward to reading more by this remarkable woman and thank her for enlightening me about the difficulties faced by members of the LGTB community.

©*Viga Boland, 2016 (Originally published at* ***http://www.vianvi.com)***

BACK TO LIFE

A memoir by Kathy McLaughlin
http://www.kmclaughlin.com/book/

Do you know how it feels to have everything in your career, family and love life humming along, as if you were on a magic carpet ride and then, suddenly, have the rug pulled out from under you? I sure do. That happened to me when I was 50, just as it happened for Kathy McLaughlin in **Back to Life**. The reasons we both crash-landed were medical, different for both of us, but after reading what happened to Kathy at only 40, I think I was the luckier of the two.

As Kathy tells us in **Back to Life**, at the time her story opens, she was the Vice President of the western division of the Rogers Communication empire, and as such, she was one very busy woman, wife and the mother of two young children. Kathy often guilt-tripped about not spending enough time with her family as a result of 16-hour working days and business trips out of town, but she loved her job, the lifestyle it afforded her family, and the challenges it presented to her workaholic, type A personality. There wasn't much time for herself either, and when all hell broke loose with the news she had Hodgkin's Disease, ie. cancer, she had to ask herself how much had she contributed to this horrible diagnosis.

What follows in **Back to Life** is Kathy's recounting of months, and later years of her efforts, and those of medical teams to keep her alive. To Kathy and her family's joy, the many months of chemo killed off the cancer and Kathy climbed right back onto that magic carpet with a new job and renewed energy. She resumed her workaholic way of life. But several years later, she crash-landed once again, this time much harder and much worse than before: the cancer was back and along with it, a liver nearly destroyed by the previous chemo treatments. This is when the real battle began: the doctors didn't dare do more chemo because of what it would do to Kathy's liver. The liver needed to be treated or replaced first. Now the hunt was on for a liver donation while the cancer continued to grow.

Anyone who has faced a life-threatening disease, especially cancer, will want to read **Back to Life** by Kathy McLaughlin, not just for what you will learn about treatments, both medical and alternative, but to be spiritually and mentally uplifted by the author's positive, take charge approach to her health. The tough business executive she is served her well when it came to fighting for her life, and she shares many of her thoughts and approaches with those willing to learn and be inspired.

The best way to describe **Back to Life** is this is a book for winners by a winner. Those who aren't prepared to just sit back, give in to what seems inevitable and let the medics do their thing will just feel overwhelmed by what Kathy has had to endure. But those with a winning, "I can get on top of this", "I'm not going down without a fight" attitude will love and agree with what Kathy McLaughlin and I both know: healing begins in the mind. Great book!

©*Viga Boland, 2016. As reviewed for*
http://www.readersfavorite.com

NOT THE BODY

A biographical memoir by Shirlie K. Plomer

Not The Body by Shirlie K. Plomer is almost too unbelievable to be true crime or memoir. Several times I checked the category under which it was listed to be sure I hadn't made a mistake: surely it was fiction. But no, no mistake. **Not The Body** is actually a memoir of true crime...unbelievable, riveting, alarming and shrouded in mystery...not just about the crime itself, but about whose memoir this is. It's not Shirlie K. Plomer's. Or, put it another way, that's what the author would have us believe. Don't you just love a mystery? **Not The Body** is certainly that.

The story is the untold and deeply hidden events of a true crime shared with Shirlie K. Plomer by a popular and very wealthy female author who lived to be 108 years old. Go ahead. Google famous female authors who lived that long and see if you can find her. I already did and can't. So one comes away from **Not The Body** even more curious about the goodies and the baddies in this memoir.

According to Shirlie K. Plomer, this famous author, who goes by a pen name of Madeline Cruise in the book, asked Shirlie to write **Not The Body**, but swore her to secrecy. Set in Australia, which happens to be Shirlie K. Plomer's homeland, Madeline Cruise is in her eighties when a bedraggled beggar appears at her front door. Madeline, a generous, loving woman, feels compelled to give him some food and clean him up, and when she does, she realizes to her shock that this beggar is her long estranged son. Overjoyed at being reunited with him, what happens after he reveals that he has just been released from solitary confinement for the murder of his wife and children 15 years earlier has the reader holding their breath and rapidly turning pages.

The reason for all the hush-hush around the true identity of Madeline Cruise is to protect her family and the families of 15 victims of kidnapping, horrendous sexual abuse, and depravity in the highest levels of society and the police force. In **Not The Body**, the reader will learn about the ultimate and clever capture of the real monster behind the supposed murder of Madeline's family, for which her son was wrongly convicted. Without disclosing too much, I can tell you that this Madeline Cruise, whoever she was, was one amazing and very strong woman whose love for her son and determination to get to the truth saved so many others from what would have been certain death. And what a character she is! Shirlie K. Plomer has a done a great job in capturing her indomitable spirit, her sense of humour, and her deeply spiritual side. The only frustration I feel with **Not The Body** is not knowing the real identity of Madeline Cruise...which is exactly what she wanted.

Prepare to be shocked, even nauseated at times with what you will read. I guarantee you will come away, as I did, more curious than ever about who, what, when, where and why!

©Viga Boland, 2016. As reviewed for
http://www.readersfavorite.com

WHERE CHILDREN RUN

A biographical memoir by Karen Emilson for David and Dennis Domko

http://www.karenemilson.com

As a victim of child abuse myself, I have a pretty thick skin when I read stories similar to my own. But **Where Children Run** by Karen Emilson shook me to my core with its depiction of violence against children, especially since **Where Children Run** is a true story.

There were times this tough-skinned reviewer audibly winced and had to put the book down to catch her breath as these young children ran for their lives into the freezing bushes or lakes during Manitoba winters to avoid yet another brutal beating by their Polish stepfather, Boleslaw Domko. The man was, as we learn at the end of the book, schizophrenic, as well as paranoid, selfish, insanely jealous and childish. His wife Caroline, a Catholic turned Jehovah's Witness was unable to stand up to him for her children or herself. And compounding her inability to act were the dictates of her religion.

Events are seen primarily through the eyes of the twins, David and Dennis, who suffer the bulk of the horrific abuse at Domko's hands. Why does he hate these children so much? Because they are not his own. His treatment of them is in sharp contrast to how he treats the children Caroline bears him. Mind you, in one of his rages, he even throws his natural baby daughter into a wall. The result is blindness. While he regrets that and treats her with love as she grows, he has no remorse for starving the other children, working them mercilessly from a very young age on their farm, throwing pitchforks and shooting at them with the intention of killing them.

These children are terrorized for over 12 years. How they survive and live to tell the tale through the help of kindly neighbors, a persistent social worker and eventually through the author, Karen Emilson, is a marvel. But above all it's a testament to the strength of the human spirit, of our instincts for survival. Readers will agonize for the twins and their older and younger siblings; they will be infuriated by the inability of law enforcement to protect the children from Domko; they will be disgusted by religious beliefs that allow such evil abuse to continue because the man is the head of the household; and they will shake their heads in disbelief at how Domko fools other adults into believing that the children are the bad ones in this family and he is only doing his fatherly duties in disciplining them.

Where Children Run by Karen Emilson is eye-opening, revolting, disturbing and sadly, true. David and Dennis agreed as teens if they survived their ordeals, they would one day tell their story. **Where Children Run** is their story. But it's unfortunately, the story of thousands of other abused children worldwide. Read it ... if you dare and care.

©Viga Boland, 2016. As reviewed for http://www.readersfavorite.com

FAR AND AWAY

An Autobiographical Travel Memoir by Russell Sunshine

When you're too old, or don't have the finances needed to travel the world, you can do several things: you can watch TV travel documentaries; go online and read thousands of articles on places you'd like to visit or even cross oceans and walk city streets using Google Earth. There's only one problem with all of those: none of them will take you inside the cultures, customs and hearts of the people living there. That's what Russell Sunshine does for you with his wonderful travel memoirs in **Far and Away**.

What a treasure and pleasure it is to read the 50 true tales Russell Sunshine shares. And yes, that is his actual name. Even the story he tells about how he came to have that last name is an entertaining read, as are just about all the stories **Far and Away**.

As an independent policy advisor in his adult years, Russell travels through East Africa, India, China, Polynesia, just to name a few countries, encountering all kinds of people and politics, rogues and unfamiliar customs. His sense of humor, even when facing danger is infectious. His intellectual and political savvy is enviable. His sensitivity to human suffering is heartfelt and memorable. The reader comes away with a great sense of satisfaction and many times more knowledgeable about those who do not live and think as we do. What we discover is often surprising but important if we are to better understand those not just outside, but within our own communities.

Far and Away is beautifully laid out and includes maps to orient us during Russell Sunshine's journeys. What adds an even richer element to this book are the large, included photos, dating all the way back to the days of his grandfather in the early 1900's. Costumes, uniforms, ships and locations come to life in more than words as one peruses the pictures.

But make no mistake: Russell Sunshine's way with words is superb. He captures deep emotions in himself and others as deftly as he does the scenery of the landscapes through which he travels. We sense the fear of his female comrades as they are being groped in a jam-packed marketplace in India. We identify with Russell's puzzlement about Laotian's seeming passivity and restraint and we feel the pain and anger of the artist who survived life in the Gulag.

But before Russell Sunshine takes us across the continents, he eases our way into his life and personality by sharing his antics as a young child voyaging with his mother, and later as one of a group of adventurous teens stuck on cliff-face and unable to climb down. As an adult, despite including the occasional heady political and economical negotiations Russell faces in his career, once this author has hooked us, this memoir is nearly impossible to put down.

Want to experience the world but can't? Pick up **Far and Away** and start exploring the real depths of our world in a way you'll never see on Google Earth!

©*Viga Boland, 2016. As reviewed for*
http://www.readersfavorite.com

CHANGE YOUR NAME AND DISAPPEAR

A memoir by Rosie Malezer

It's not every day that I read a book and come away impressed, not just by the writer and the writing, but by the person behind the events, in this case, Rosie Malezer.

Change Your Name and Disappear was the advice Rosie was given after she had been threatened with death by her fiance, a violent, somewhat deranged and utterly controlling man who nearly killed her during one of his rages. Her efforts to change her name and disappear took her thousands of miles from her birth home in Australia and eventually landed her in Finland, where Rosie Malezer did meet and marry a good man. But by that time, she was almost completely deaf, thanks to the last beating her fiance had dealt her, and eventually, she was also declared legally blind.

Even though "Change Your Name and Disappear" could benefit from somewhat tighter editing, along with more dialogue and less narrative at times, Rosie Malezer's true story is riveting and readers will find they can't put the book down. But as compelling as the story is, it is Rosie Malezer herself who grabs you, especially when you research her online and see just how many books she has written despite her sensory handicaps of deafness and blindness. This woman is driven to prove to herself and the world that has abused her, in more ways than can be shared in this review, just how strong and wonderful she really is. And she succeeds. I find myself in utter awe of her achievements and motivation to continue achieving where others would have given up long ago. What an inspiration Rosie Malezer is!

Rosie's next book, **How to be Deaf** is about to hit the stores and I know it's going to be amazing. How do I know that? Because of what Rosie herself says on her blog about it: "After living as a profoundly Deaf woman for the past 15 months, when weighing up the pros and the cons, I would definitely choose Deaf over hearing any day."

Okay Rosie. You've got me. I just have to find out why you would say that! Given my husband is now about 90% deaf and at nearly 70 years of age, I can expect my hearing to wane soon too,

I know your upcoming book is on my "must read" list. But in the meantime, readers of this review need to pick up **Change Your Name and Disappear** and get to know Rosie Malezer. You'll be glad you did.

©*Viga Boland, 2016. As reviewed for*
http://www.readersfavorite.com

"IT'S NOT ABOUT THE SEX", MY ASS: CONFESSIONS OF AN EX MORMON, EX POLYGAMIST, EX WIFE

A Memoir by Joanne Hanks
http://www.itsnotaboutthesexmyass.com

I'll be honest: I was drawn to this book by its outrageous title. It also helped to read a write up that indicated that the author was taking a humorous approach to a serious subject ... and polygamy justified in the name of religion is pretty serious. As someone who has herself written a memoir on a very serious subject, I just had to see how one could write "funny" about something sad.

Joanne Hanks had me turning pages in no time. Her opening chapter was riveting. She was laughing and I laughed with her, but it didn't take long to realize that what I was laughing at wasn't really funny. I couldn't put the book down as she detailed her life as a wife in a Mormon sect where having the husband take more and more wives guaranteed them both eternal happiness. And amazingly, she was going along with it, asking me to believe she was fine with her husband getting it on with different women each night of the week if it meant eternal salvation for them both. But bit by bit, over the years, as she got older and the "sister wives" got younger and younger, Joanne began to see this practice for what it really was, an excuse for her husband to enjoy himself being fruitful and multiplying to build the cult. "Not about the sex?" Ha!

I don't want to tell you too much more about what happened to Joanne and her husband, their children, their position in the church, but I will tell you that once they broke away, Joanne and hubby became big news in the media. They also got divorced. Why am I not surprised?

Toward the end of the book, Joanne writes *"Cults are horrible things. Worse, they make you afraid to trust your common sense. Here is the best protection from charlatans, manipulators, controllers and opportunists I can offer: whenever you find your emotions pulling you toward believing the opposite of what the evidence says, overrule your emotions and trust the evidence. There is no better way to spare yourself the pain of needless, unfortunate decisions."*

Joanne is right. She's also my kind of writer, one who doesn't waste the reader's time, padding the facts with unnecessary detail that doesn't move the story along. Not all of us have time, or even want to analyze characters. Some of us just like an absorbing, quick read that enlightens us to worlds and societies unlike those in which we live. This is what Joanne gives us in this book and she's done it all with humor. How very clever!

©*Viga Boland, originally published in Memoirabilia magazine*

NOT IN THE PINK

An illustrated, artistic memoir by Tina Martel
http://www.notinthepink.ca

Not in the Pink by Tina Martel is the most stunning and unusual memoir I have ever seen or read. Why do I say "seen"? Because when you read **Not in the Pink** you actually SEE Tina Martel's journey from her discovery of breast cancer, through to her chemo-therapy and radiation treatments to her questionable recovery from both the physical and mental pain of the entire experience.

The reader sees this journey because Tina Martel is an artist. The page backgrounds of her memoir are paintings and photographs that illustrate what she is saying or describing in the text. Readers find themselves pouring over the details in the graphics while they read the words depicting her long and difficult battle with the cancer, the treatment, the meds and sadly, the attitudes of hospital staff and others along the way. This is not a page-turner in the regular sense of the word because one feels compelled to explore the illustrations before moving on to the next page. The entire concept is brilliant, a visual and writing feast for the eyes that leaves the reader seeing and remembering **Not in the Pink** long after the reading has ended.

According to an article published in 2014 by the Grand Prairie Daily Herald-Tribune, Tina Martel feels "there are many myths surrounding breast cancer" including that it's not as difficult as other cancers. Well, she certainly debunks that myth in **Not in the Pink**. My reaction to what I was reading and after I'd finished was I hope I never have to go through what Tina Martel and so many other women do. There is nothing easy about breast cancer or the treatment of it. As Tina says, "It's a profound and life-changing experience". And yet, throughout the memoir, Tina has found moments to laugh at herself and her circumstances and share those with her readers.

I, for one, will never forget Tina Martel and how she has chosen to share her memoir, **Not in the Pink**. Consider me a lifelong fan of this artist and writer. Bravo!

©Viga Boland, originally published in Memoirabilia magazine

TWO DECADES of DIAPERS

A memoir by Barbara Studham
http://www.barbarastudham.com

When you're a victim of child sexual abuse, as I was, it's startling to read another person's memoir and find it disturbs you more than your own story, especially when it's based on a different kind of horror: fetal alcohol syndrome. But that's how I felt reading Barbara Studham's **Two Decades of Diapers**.

Knowing Barbara personally, I was aware of some details of her life, but I wasn't prepared for what I read in this book. I came away not only feeling very sorry for what she has had to live with for 20 years, but also incredibly impressed by her strength. Barbara's courage and stamina reminds me of that rather funny adage: a woman is like a tea bag: she doesn't know how strong she is until you put her in hot water.

Barbara began steeping in hot water when she decided to adopt her own 15-year-old daughter's first baby. She went on to adopt another three of the seven children her daughter birthed and left for others to look after. The others went to foster homes and to this day, Barbara has little or no contact with this wayward daughter.

Little did Barbara realize, when she took on the role of being a mother to her four grandchildren, how difficult it is to raise and deal with children afflicted with fetal alcohol syndrome. Barbara's grandchildren were developmentally, socially and mentally challenged. They did things like smearing excrement all over their bedroom walls or setting fires around the house. They forgot things almost as soon as they were told them, lost things, and needed 24 hour supervision. Unmarried, Barbara had no-one to help or relieve her. As a result, now 20 years later, she has become almost a recluse, desperately in need of a break and deserving of some joy.

I'm sure Barbara has found occasional joy in being a grandmother to these children, but from an objective point of view, perhaps the best thing that's come from all this is her important book, **Two Decades of Diapers.** Barbara has had ample time to reflect on what it's like to raise FAS children and as much as this book is memoir, it's also a reference book for others in the same situation. Barbara's memoir style is conversational, but in the latter part of the book, still in an easy to follow tone, she shares valuable information on all aspects of FAS.

The part of **Two Decades of Diapers** that hit me hardest occurred near the end, where Barbara almost begs relatives, teachers, grocery clerks, mothers and fathers to realize just how hurtful their behavior and attitudes toward such challenged children are, not just to Barbara, but to the children themselves. These children didn't deserve the lot life dealt them because their mother chose to drink while they grew inside her. They also don't deserve what they now endure daily as they grow and cope with life outside the womb.

I could say so much more but I'll leave it at suggesting you read **Two Decades of Diapers** if fetal alcohol syndrome is something you worry about. This fine book is hard to put down and what you read will stay with you long after you read the last page. Congratulations Barbara Studham on your first memoir. Bravo!

FETAL ALCOHOL SYNDROME:
THE TEEN YEARS

A follow-up memoir by Barbara Studham
http://www.barbarastudham.com

Is your teenager forever getting into trouble at school or sometimes not even going? Is he hanging with friends you know aren't good company? Is your daughter freaking out, having meltdowns or screaming hissy fits over the smallest issues? Has your child always had learning difficulties, been diagnosed with ADHD and put on meds? And are you getting worn out trying to control a child who is forever out of control?

Perhaps the reason you're not getting suitable answers for your questions or non-medicating solutions to such behavioral problems from doctors and others who should know what to do is that these professionals aren't recognizing the full-blown signs of Fetal Alcohol Syndrome...and neither are you. In that case, both Barbara Studham's books on FASD should be required reading for medical and behavioral professionals, as well as parents like you. All the research done so far will not enlighten you as much as these first-hand accounts of raising four children with FASD from infants to teenagers.

In Barbara's first book, **Two Decades of Diapers** she covered how she gradually came to recognize that the behavior she was dealing with in the four grandchildren she adopted, was actually the behavior of children who were mentally challenged thanks to their birth mother drinking throughout her pregnancy. Years of wiping her children's feces from the walls of her home gave way to dealing with teens who shoplifted, got high with friends, ignored and swore at her for reasonable requests and in the end, just became too much for a single grandmother to continue handling alone after 22 years.

Barbara recounts her sleepless nights, discomfort with curious and critical neighbors, police and CAS workers, all the while trying to get everyone to realize these children weren't just badly raised kids: they were mentally challenged, and as such, needed much greater understanding and different handling than what most services offer. This is no case of one size fits all, or what worked for one will work for another.

Throughout both books, the reader will feel the enormous

love, mingled with desperation and worry that Barbara has for her four grandchildren. But her books are more than just memoirs of her experiences: they offer solid advice on where and how to get help for children with FASD, along with a warning of the difficulties one faces in getting proper help.

While this is supposed to be a review of the second book, FASD, the Teen Years, it's essential that those seeking information on FASD read both Barbara's books. Just as she does in "Two Decades of Diapers", Barbara writes this second book in an easy to read, personal tone that makes you feel you are simply hearing her story while having a coffee with her. She doesn't preach or talk down to you: she just pours out her heart. But what she has to share is invaluable knowledge in an up close an personal look at teenagers who end up suffering the consequences of alcohol consumption during pregnancy. Both Barbara's books will make those hoping to have children think twice about that night of drinking, or even that one glass of wine followed by intimacy when hoping to conceive.

That said, I'm sure Barbara's purpose in writing these books isn't to frighten but to enlighten. Barbara Studham wants to increase awareness of a subject, Fetal Alcohol Syndrome, that demands much more intensive research than it has been given to date. Along with its predecessor, **Two Decades of Diapers** and **FASD the Teen Years** should be required reading for all parents, parents to be and professionals because children matter.

©*Viga Boland. The two preceding reviews were originally published in Memoirabilia magazine in 2015*

SPLIT

A memoir by Mary Dispenza
http://www.marydispenza.com

Split, the true story of a child, a priest and the Catholic church by Mary Dispenza rocked my world for two reasons: first, I attended Catholic schools till I was 18; secondly, I was, like Mary, a victim of child sexual abuse.

But if **Split** rocked my world, it might just turn the worlds of millions of devout Catholics upside down. Those are the followers who still deny, or refuse to believe this could be happening, despite all the reports of childhood abuse by priests, not to mention the Church's failure to protect innocent children by removing such predators from places where they will still have contact with youngsters.

It is just such a story that Mary Dispenza shares with us in **Split.** Molested...no, let's use the right word...raped repeatedly by Father Rucker from the age of 7, Mary split in two psychologically. She was well into her 30's or older when she began to recognize why she was incapable of loving and/or having sexual relationships without feeling shame. When she finally came to grips with what had happened to her at such a young age. and just who had abused her, she barely survived the realization. Only her faith in God and the support of a woman she came to love in every way, helped her go to court and speak out against Father Rucker. In doing so, she brought some measure of justice and peace, not just to herself, but to 30 or more other children abused by Father Rucker.

What makes **Split** an even more engrossing read is the fact that Mary Dispenza became a nun at 18. In some odd, unconscious way, God became her be all and end all. But then, after years serving God as a nun, Mary left the convent. It was there that she had discovered that she was gay. Was that a consequence of the childhood abuse, or just something in her genes? Mary doesn't address that but, as an absorbing, thinking person's read, it bears speculation.

I couldn't put **Split** down. I breathed a sigh of relief at the end in finding Mary had found some measure of peace and forgiveness in her heart after all she went through, both as a child and an adult who lost jobs and almost became penniless because of religious intolerance of sexual preference.

But what I couldn't help thinking as I closed the book was "is the cover-up of sexual abuse by the religious limited to the Catholic Church?" Unfortunately, I think not. The Catholic church is easily singled out because priests are celibate. But I feel sure that such practices, both the abuse and the consequent cover-up, are rampant throughout all religious groups and institutions.

Kudos to Mary Dispenza for writing this painful memoir and expose. We need more brave women...and men...like her telling the world how it really is! As I have said in my own talks on sexual abuse, "victims voices are the best weapons against sexual abuse". Let's not silence those voices any longer.

©Viga Boland 2015. Originally published at
http://www.memoirabilia.ca

A FAR CRY...FROM HOME

A memoir by Sandy Richards
http://www.sandy-richards.com

Is there a greater tragedy for parents than the loss of a child? From what I've read on this heartbreaking topic, and from what I've learned from those who have lost a child, there isn't. And as one father told me years after his adult son died in a drowning accident, the longer that child has been in your life, the longer you've shared their dreams for their future, their achievements, their everything, the harder it is to bear that loss.

So how does one move on once the shock and grief has subsided? Like in most cases where one has to deal with trauma, journaling your pain is enormously therapeutic. That's what Sandy Richards did, after her elder son, Tyler, died in a car accident. She poured her heart out directly to Tyler, talking to him night after night, often at his gravesite. She collected all the poems, tributes, newspaper reports regarding her very popular and loved son, and then, decided to share everything with others who might be living through, and trying to escape the same hell she survived. She wrote and self-published a beautiful tribute to her son and all the friends, relatives, neighbors who supported her through the tragedy in her memoir, "A Far Cry ... from Home."

But, being a writer, along with a heart-broken mother, she put an unusual spin on the telling of this story: her narrator is her son Tyler, now an angel in heaven. What a refreshing approach, and Sandy has carried it off beautifully. Tyler comes across as alive, no doubt very much how he was most likely was during his life. We come to know Tyler as he was, and perhaps as he is now, if one believes in angels. This method of memoir works so well that the book earned Sandy an Honorable Mention in the 2014 Readers Favorite book awards.

I had the supreme pleasure of meeting Sandy and her younger son, Austin, at the Readers Favorite 2014 Book Awards ceremony. If Tyler was anything like Austin, and I'm sure he was, Sandy's love and pride in both her sons is certainly understandable. What an outstanding young man Austin is. He accompanied his mother to the awards and stood on stage with her during her acceptance. The most touching moment for me was Austin and Sandy saying Tyler was accepting the award with them. Tyler Richards is still, and always will be very much alive in their hearts and his 16 years of life will be forever celebrated in **A Far Cry...from Home.**

©Viga Boland, originally published in Memoirabilia Magazine #2

ALABAMA BLUE

A memoir by Toni K. Pacini
http://www.toni-k-pacini.com/alabama-blue.html

As someone who runs memoir writing workshops, I've always maintained that memoir, just like fiction, needs dialogue to reveal character, move the story along quickly and sustain reader interest. In **Alabama Blue,** Toni K. Pacini has shown that isn't always true. Hence, I'm still slightly shocked at how skillfully Toni K. Pacini wrote her long memoir relying 95% of the time on narrative minus dialogue, yet somehow kept me riveted!

How did she do it? Well, for starters, the details of her life, after being born "poor white trash" to a hopelessly alcoholic mother who married 7 times, are heartbreaking. This is the story of a child who grew into her teens and adulthood feeling invisible, unloved and unwanted; a person who stumbled down life's pathway mirroring her mother when it came to booze, drugs and men as she searched for love and a reason for living. Close to suicide many times, she persevered through poverty, rejection, rapes, social and religious bigotry and hypocrisy.

As much as **Alabama Blue** is a memoir, it's also a social and religious commentary. So many times I stopped and thought about the implications of what Toni was revealing about the societies, mores, beliefs, and practices of which she was a victim. I find myself sickened by much of it and most certainly understand why Alabama made her blue and she never wants to live there again. Her original title was to be "Southern Discomfort". No kidding!

While most of **Alabama Blue** is focused on the difficulties Toni. K. Pacini endured, she also shares some very funny events with her readers.

Her foray into looking for love via Craig's List had me laughing out loud. But it was the tenderness of the love she shared with her dogs, especially one named "The Goose" that had the dog lover in me identifying with her all the way: her four-legged companion gave her what human beings couldn't and didn't: unconditional love. And when Toni cries as "The Goose" dies, we cry with her. Thankfully, by that time, she has indeed found herself a good man, Walt, to help her deal with yet another loss in a life filled with loss.

At the time of publication, Toni and Walt have now been together 12 years. Over the 50 or so years before Walt, bit by bit Toni pulled herself out of the trashy world of her birth. She managed to get her GED, and support herself in her later years through various jobs, and with the help of "The Goose", learn to love herself and come to believe someone could love her back. Now in her 60's, Toni heads up writing groups in her area and is working on another book.

Alabama Blue by Toni. K. Pacini is proof of what I've always believed: "It's our attitude, and not our aptitude, that determines our altitude". Inspiring!

©*Viga Boland. Originally published at*
http://www.memoirabilia.ca

THE STOVEPIPE

A memoir by Bonnie Virag
http://www.myauthorwebsite.net/bonnie-virag

If it hadn't been for the enthusiasm with which the Simcoe bookseller spoke of **The Stovepipe**, the odds are I might never have heard of this book, let alone read it. Except for the fact that I was writing my own memoir on child sexual abuse, I'd never been particularly interested in memoirs, other than those of famous people. But when the bookseller told me that Bonnie's book, based on her childhood experiences of living in foster homes had been selling strongly for nearly 18 months, I got curious. Why was this book so successful? Was it just because it was based in the Simcoe, Ontario environs that so many locals or those who grew up there were interested? Or was it the story itself that kept bringing more and more buyers into the little shop?

It didn't take long to find my answer as to why **The Stovepipe** has sold so well. Yes, of course, the locals were interested in a story based in their city, but it was more than that. Bonnie Virag writes with the same warmth that she exudes in person. She's infectious; her eyes twinkle when she speaks, and as you read about young Bonnie and her twin sister Betty, their older sisters Jean and Joan and their brother Bobby all being torn away from their older sister "Muggs" and eventually from each other by the CSA, you're instantly won over by these children who will spend the next decade or more in and out of foster homes, not all of which really care about young children.

Removed abruptly from their earlier placement with a kindly couple, Betty and Bonnie are sent to live with the Benders, a cold family that truly makes one question why the CSA would even allow these people to be foster parents. The Benders certainly weren't doing foster care because they liked children. Obviously it was for the money they'd receive. It's not long before their equally uncaring and callous son rapes little Betty while Bonnie looks on hopelessly and helplessly. But do the children ever tell the CSA lady when she comes to check up on the family? Of course not. By that time, Jean and Joan who'd been sent to another home, have come to live with the Benders as well, and all 4 girls are locked away in a tiny, cold attic where the only warmth comes from the stovepipe. It's also their only slight connection with what is going on in the Bender family and the world, as they are never allowed to eat dinner with the Benders, not even at Christmas! During the summer holidays, living on meagre rations and so hungry they eat sassafras grass growing nearby, "because if the horses eat it, we can too!" the girls work long, hot hours on the Benders' tobacco farm, doing hard labor that would tax grown men. It's a cruel life for young girls who never really knew why they were taken from their birth mother in the first place.

But as Bonnie tells the story of their hardship, she also laces it with wonderfully warm, even humorous vignettes that capture the children's love for each other and their determination to survive. The hard work, coupled with the support and care they show each other, carries them through that tough childhood into womanhood from which they emerge not only as survivors but thrivers. Ultimately, this is the kind of story we all enjoy, one that reminds us that when the going gets tough, the tough get going and it's love that keep us together.

Today, Bonnie is in her 70's. She's a tiny little woman with an adoring and supportive husband, and when you look at her, you can't help but see little Bonnie ever looking out for her sister Betty and hanging onto the hope, that one day, things will get better. They certainly did and it's wonderful that Bonnie Virag has told us all about it in **The Stovepipe**. Easy to read and highly recommended if true life is your kind of reading.

©Viga Boland. Originally published in Memoirabilia Magazine #2

I PROMISED NOT TO TELL

A memoir by Cheryl B. Evans
http://www.writtenbymom.ca

In the closing pages of **I Promised Not To Tell** by Cheryl B. Evans, the author says she wonders if she has made a mistake in publishing this book. Let me begin by assuring her the only mistake would have been to not publish it. **I Promised Not To Tell** is quite possibly one of the most important books to date on a very controversial, and little understood social issue: transgenderism. And what makes it even more valuable is that the focus is on helping parents recognize, and whether they like it or not, accept that their daughter might actually be a son or vice versa.

To enlighten others about some of the dreadful problems associated with a child being transgender, since she promised not to tell, Cheryl B. Evans has had to use fictitious names for real people. The real people in this story are members of her own family. **I Promised Not To Tell** is about Cheryl's daughter, Jordan, whose transition from female to male begins around the time of puberty. Had the parents ignored or dismissed the warning signs that things just weren't right for Jordan at that time, this story would most likely have had an unwanted and tragic ending.

But as Cheryl B. Evans states early in **I Promised Not To Tell**, and repeats throughout the book, what she and her husband wanted most for her children was their happiness. And everything these parents do in this book proves they mean what they say. They listened to, and trusted in what Jordan believed was right for her; they educated themselves on transgenderism; they located knowledgeable therapists and doctors, and stood united and strong beside their daughter when faced with religious ignorance that claims such children are "not of God".

Cheryl B. Evans has documented each life-changing step of Jordan's transition from female to male so that others who may be facing the same issues and don't know where to turn have a place to start, coupled with the knowledge they are not alone. Cheryl addresses issues like washroom use, dating in later years and the gender affirming surgeries more frequently called sex reassignment. At the end of the book she includes a list of resources and contacts, including the names of doctors her family worked with.

Other issues raised by Cheryl are the complications that arise with simple day to day things like passports, birth certificates, driving licences etc. Think of all the official forms we fill out daily that ask us to identify ourselves as M or F. Well, what happens when M is now F? This paperwork can take months, years to change over. And on deeper levels, Cheryl makes one look at the ramifications of dating, falling in love, and falling out of love with someone who knows your secret and then tells all your mutual friends. Again, we face another social situation where people are forced to hide their true selves. As if there isn't enough cover up of so much in our world already.

I'm sure it's Cheryl's hope that, if nothing else, **I Promised Not To Tell** will open a few more minds, clarify the myths and falsehoods, and get more people talking openly about what being transgender really means. If you are facing such a situation with your child, I urge you to read this book. Both you and your child need what Cheryl has so kindly shared with readers and parents. And when you do, I'm sure you will come away impressed not just by the courage shown by Jordan in this book, but by the love Cheryl and her husband have for their children. That love affirms what I've always believed: true love has nothing to do with gender. Love is love. I loved **I Promised Not To Tell**. Highly recommended reading.

©*Viga Boland. Originally published and podcast on http://www.memoirabilia.ca*

THIS BRINGS US TO THE END OF REVIEWS OF ACTUAL MEMOIRS I THINK YOU MIGHT LIKE TO READ.

BUT ON THE FOLLOWING PAGES, I GIVE YOU TWO REVIEWS OF BOOKS ABOUT MEMOIR WRITING THAT YOU WILL FURTHER HELP WITH YOUR MEMOIR WRITING ASPIRATIONS.

THIS IS FOLLOWED BY RECOMMENDED READING AND ONLINE SITES YOU MIGHT LIKE TO VISIT FOR MORE INFORMATION ON HOW TO WRITE MEMOIR.

One More Thing:

If you've written a novel or memoir and are looking for an honest review, please check out my site at
http://www.vianvi.com
for information on my book reviewing services.

WRITING ALCHEMY
By Matilda Butler and Kendra Bonnet
http://www.womensmemoirs.com

You want to write your memoir but where do you start? Perhaps, you think you'll do what I did i.e. just pick up your pen and let it flow. Well that does work for some but such a "dive-in and get-wet" approach doesn't work for everyone, and in hindsight, my own book might have been a better book if I'd had "Writing Alchemy" on my desk.

Now, there's a wealth of books about writing memoir available on Amazon, and I have at least 10 of them. Perhaps you do too and still don't know where to start. Then buy one more book: Writing Alchemy. What Matilda Butler and Kendra Bonnett advise here supports everything you'll read in those books, but includes one step the others don't: writing a synopsis, just like your teacher used to make you do before you started that high school essay.

I can hear you groaning now as we did then. Doesn't that extra effort slow you down and add more to your writing load? Actually, if anything, it cuts back on the load and reduces your editing time at the end. I'm all for making editing easier and less time-consuming, and the process of "deconstruction" using a synopsis approach to your scenes, the chapters, the characters, events and eventually the entire story-line will do just that for you. As I finished studying the samples and completing the supplied exercises, I wondered how I'd never thought of this approach in the first place.

"Alchemy is a form of science" write the authors. Science is full of formulae and here's the one for writing a memoir:

Character + Emotion + Dialogue + Senses + (Time & Place) = Well-Written Story

Using the deconstruction/synopsis method can turn that scientific formula above into an original work of art: your memoir. Isn't that what you want for your memoir? You can have it. Buy "Writing Alchemy" today, and do sign up to receive newsletters from http://www.womensmemoirs.com. Matilda and Kendra offer so much motivation and inspiration to all who want to write memoirs. Lots of prompts and contests too!

©Viga Boland. Originally published in Memoirabilia Magazine #1, Jan 2015

DON'T LET WRITER'S BLOCK STOP YOU:
Learn techniques to sustain your writing, become motivated again, find a better fit for writing in your life. (A Memoir Network Writing Series Book 3)

By Denis Ledoux
http://www.thememoirnetwork.com

As someone who facilitates memoir writing workshops and is also currently writing her third memoir, I'm all too familiar with writer's block: I get it and so do those who participate in my workshops. And when writers block makes you throw your pen down and ask yourself why you're even trying to write, that's when you need Denis Ledoux' latest book, "Don't let Writer's Block Stop you."

This is a quick, easy read but it's full of useful advice on how to free yourself and start writing again. I got ideas from this book that i can't wait to share with members of my workshop. As I read about "task-oriented writers" I recognized members in my workshop who are, as Denis describes, so "rational, logical writers who are pursuing their need to be orderly and sequential" that their writing lacks spontaneity. Such writing so often fails to do what Denis says here, i.e. "... writing should sound as if it had spilled out on the page rather than was painfully labored over for a long time." I find this is especially true when writing memoir. Denis points out that we shouldn't rush the writing; instead we should linger with our stories so we can feel our way through the writing, just as we would linger on and gaze at a beautiful sunset.

But in case you think this book is a list of do's and don'ts, it isn't. Denis Ledoux not only makes some great suggestions for getting out of the writer's block, but ends each chapter with actual exercises. These exercises should be kept handy for those times the dreaded block grabs a hold of your pen. They alone will get the pen moving again.

An excellent, quick, and utterly resourceful book from a highly qualified teacher of memoir writing, "Don't let Writer's Block Stop You" should be added to your "Must Read" list immediately. Wait! Don't just add it to your list: Buy it now!

©Viga Boland. Originally published in Memoirabilia Magazine #1, Jan 2015

THE FINAL WORD ON WHAT NOT TO DO WHEN WRITING A MEMOIR

By BlueInk Review
(Reprinted with Permission)

You've lived an interesting and full life – and now you want to leave a legacy. It's time to write your memoirs.

This is a laudable goal, and many, many authors have amazing stories to tell. But too often, they don't deliver the sort of book readers at large can appreciate. At BlueInk Review, we've vetted nearly 1,000 independently published memoirs, written by people from all walks of life. In the process, we've become experts on where authors go wrong when tackling a memoir.

Here are 6 of the most common mistakes we see authors making:

1. They try to settle old grudges.

Many of the memoirs we receive read more like a list of grievances than an artful telling of the author's life. While scores of wonderful memoirs portray terrible injustices (think *Angela's Ashes*), these grievances are an organic part of the story, shown through the actions of the characters, rather than directly spelled out for readers. Furthermore, skilled authors bring new and interesting insights to these old injustices, as they reflect from the distance of time and perspective.

No one wants to read the work of someone who seems petty and bitter. If you have past hurts to settle, close your laptop and call a therapist. You'll likely get better results—and you'll spare the rest of us from having to read all about your personal grudges.

2. They try to mention every person they ever met.

Sure, someone's feelings may get hurt if you leave them out of your story, but you need to ask yourself: Am I writing this for the people I've met in my life, or for a general audience? If the answer is the latter, then throwing in endless names of those who don't play a key role in the story will alienate your audience, who will begin to feel as if reading the phone book might be just as interesting as continuing to plow through your book.

3. They start at birth and mention every life event in chronological order.

No doubt the easiest way to approach a memoir is to start at birth and move chronologically to the present. But this rarely makes for the most engaging storytelling. Successful memoirs start with gripping scenes that may reference the beginning of the author's life, but just as likely occur somewhere in the middle and even the end. (Think, *The Glass Castle*, which begins when the author is an adult, working for *The New York Times*; looking out the window of her taxi, she sees her mother rummaging through a dumpster. Now *that's* a beginning!) Remember: your task is to tell an interesting story, not just to chronicle every moment of your life from start to finish. Leave out inconsequential events and keep in mind that you're building a story, not just making a list.

4. Worse than No. 3, they don't organize the book at all.

Writing chronologically is immensely better than no organization at all. We often see memoirs by authors who have simply jotted down random memories as they come to them, leading to chaos on the page—and readers who discard the book long before reaching its end.

5. They lack artful writing.

Successful memoirs aren't just a chronicle of events that, together, add up to the sum total of a person's life. They are written with artful prose that often uses metaphor, simile, vivid descriptions and other compelling writing techniques. In addition, they offer keen insights, hard won by the author, into events long past. By contrast, many of the memoirs we receive are written in a chatty style that might appeal to those who know the author, but don't offer the universal messages and fine writing that would attract a wider readership.

6. They expect a bestseller when the book is best viewed as a family keepsake.

There's nothing wrong with cataloging your life as a document to leave to family and friends. The mistake independently publishing authors often make is in thinking these documents will be of interest to those outside their inner circle. Take stock of your story and level with yourself: Would you be interested in it if you hadn't written it? If you're an accountant who has led a run-of-the-mill life, the answer is likely "no." If so, print 50 copies for your family and friends — and save yourself the regret of looking at stacks of unsold books sitting in the shadow of rakes and old bicycles every time you open the garage door.

BlueInk Review is a fee-based book review service devoted to self-published titles exclusively. For more news and writing and marketing tips, sign up for our mailing list. And be sure and visit us at

http://www.blueinkreview.com

RECOMMENDED READING:

How to Write a Best Selling Memoir by Victoria Twead

Lifetales Workbook by Karen Hamilton Silvestri

Naked, Drunk and Driving by Adair Lara

Writing Your Legacy by Richard Campbell & Cheryl Svensson

The Memoir Revolution by Jerry Waxler

Should I write my Memoir by Denis Ledoux

Fiction Writing Modes by Mike Klaassen

Writing Alchemy by Matilda Butler and Kendra Bonnett

Writing Without a Parachute by Barbara Turner Vesselago

On Writing: A memoir of the Craft by Stephen King

The Memoir Project by Marion Roach Smith

Story Genius by Lisa Cron

Story Trumps. Structure by Stephen James

GO MEMOIR WRITING SITE-SEEING:

http://www.thememoirnetwork.com

http://www.womensmemoirs.com

http://www.jerrywaxler.com

http://www.marionroach.com

http://www.memoirabilia.ca

http://www.namw.com

ABOUT THE AUTHOR

I've always had a love affair with the power of words. Words can build us up or tear us down in seconds. Whichever way they are used, there are lifelong ramifications for all who read or hear them.

As a victim of child sexual abuse, I know all too well how harsh, unkind words can destroy self-esteem. Today, as an aging survivor and thriver, I want the words I speak and write to motivate and inspire others to explore their talents and realize their dreams, as I have mine. I hope that all who read my books, even my disturbing memoirs will take away the positives I've presented in all of them.

Although all my books are available through the usual popular online distributors, and I appreciate all purchases, I'm very grateful to those of you who purchase my books directly from my author's site at **http://www.vigaboland.com**. *You see, I'm completely self-published. While I'll never get rich or famous by being self-published, your direct purchases help recoup some of the costs I incur in self publishing and promotion.*

When I'm not writing books, I am busy reading and reviewing books for other writers and offer my book reviewing services via my site at **http://www.vianvi.com**. *As long as I am able, I will continue to mentor and promote other memoir writers via my podcasts from both the sites above and from my memoir writers' site at* **http://www.memoirabilia.ca**

I would most appreciate your referrals to other writers for **"Don't Write Your MEmoir without ME!"** *along with your reviews which can be left on my websites or on the various online distributor sites.*

Thanks for reading this book and this page. Here are the titles of all my books:

No Tears for my Father *(a true story of incest)*
Learning to Love Myself *(recovery and self-discovery after abuse)*
Voice from an Urn *(my mother's side of my true story)*
The Ladies of Loretto *(a humorous memoir of 4 years in a Catholic Girls School in the 60's)*
Love Has No Gender *(a short, fictional love story with an unexpected twist)*
Don't Write Your MEmoir without ME! *(a motivational workbook for memoir writer writers)*

With love and gratitude,
Viga Boland, B.A.

A Reflection On Writing Memoir

A page a day
Makes a 365 page book

Look at the photos in your mind
Feel the people behind
the smiles
behind the tears
Recall their fears
What they said

Share with us the words they bled
Onto the pages of your life
Let others see their lives through yours:
The strife, the pain
Finding joy again

Write that memoir
Speak the past
In a voice so strong
It's heard long
after the book is done

Just let it flow
Go where it wants to go
A page a day
Come the setting sun
A sigh of relief
Another page done

©Viga Boland, 2015

www.ingramcontent.com/pod-product-compliance
Lightning Source LLC
Chambersburg PA
CBHW072006040426
42447CB00009B/1510